What Is God Like?

**Books in the Life-Transforming Truths
from a Never-Changing God Series**

Other Books by D. James Kennedy

What Is God Like?

*Life-Transforming Truths
from a Never-Changing God*

Book 1

D. James Kennedy

Fleming H. Revell
A Division of Baker Book House Co
Grand Rapids, Michigan 49516

Published by Fleming H. Revell
a division of Baker Book House Company
P.O. Box 6287, Grand Rapids, MI 49516-6287

Printed in the United States of America

Library of Congress Cataloging-in-Publication Data

Kennedy, D. James (Dennis James), 1930–
    Life-transforming truths from a never-changing God /
D. James Kennedy.
      p.   cm.
    ISBN 0-8007-5558-8 (bk. 1)
    ISBN 0-8007-5557-X (bk. 2)
    ISBN 0-8007-5559-6 (bk. 3)
    Contents: bk. 1. What is God Like? — bk. 2. How do I
get to know God? — bk. 3. How do I live for God?
    1. Theology, Doctrinal—Popular works. 2. Christian life.
3. Westminster Confession of Faith. 4. Fundamentalist
churches—Doctrines. I. Title.
[BT77.K2767   1995]
  230'.044—dc20   94-179918

Contents

Introduction

It had been "one of those days" for the nine disciples.

Peter, James, and John had gone off for a mountaintop experience with the Lord. They were seeing Jesus' glory as God partly unveiled, an experience offered to few human beings on this earth. If I had been one of the other disciples I would have felt left out and put-upon, for they were left to look after all the crowd who followed Jesus wherever he went. The disciples were slogging it out in the trenches of ministry.

To make matters worse, they were doing none too well. The immediate problem was a distraught man who had come to them, leading or carrying a little boy. "It is my son. He is troubled by a demonic spirit. Please help me!"

And they had tried. They had seen Jesus heal countless people. They knew his authority over spirits. They had used that authority when he sent them out on a preaching mission. But their commands had no effect whatsoever against the force that obviously afflicted this child.

Finally Jesus returned. Through Mark 9 we can almost see Jesus as he reached the bottom of the mountain. He surveyed the frustrated disciples, the milling

people, and the boy's father—who by now was losing
all hope.

"O faithless generation," Jesus told them. "How long
shall I suffer you? Bring him unto me."

The father eagerly approached and told the sad story
of his son's misery, asking that Jesus take pity, "if you
can do anything."

The father received a rebuking challenge in reply:
"All things are possible to him that believeth."

"I believe," the father responded, then added in hon-
esty, "help thou mine unbelief."

Do you ever feel like that man? I do. As a minister
I often feel empathy for those disciples who had their
own problems with unbelief. They experienced many
wonders as followers of Jesus. Love and power were
exhibited in the sandaled rabbi who walked beside
them. But they couldn't grasp who Jesus was. As they
slowly understood more they were able to say with new
consciousness: "I believe."

I believe, but help!

Only after the cross had unveiled God's plan, after
Jesus had broken the bonds of death, after he had
ascended to his eternal glory, after the Spirit of God
had taken permanent dwelling inside of them—did the
apostles truly turn the world upside-down. But even
then these transformed witnesses to the glory of God
echoed that father's humble prayer: "I believe; help
thou mine unbelief." And lest we forget, one of those
disciples—a sad fellow named Judas—saw Jesus'
power and love expressed. He refused to embrace him,
save as a traitor.

If you cannot say the first part of that prayer, "I
believe," or if you aren't sure, then please read on. I

was thinking of you when I wrote the following chapters. If you have rejected God you owe it to yourself to know whom and what you are rejecting. I firmly believe these truths can be a turning point that will revolutionize your life.

But if you stand with the trembling, believing father, this book also is addressed directly to you, for this series of three studies contains the *credo* of life as a disciple. The word *credo* is a venerably ancient Latin verb. It means "I believe." If you know Christ personally, I want to suggest a couple of things to you.

First, your proper goal has become the lifelong spiritual quest toward "credo."

In Christ you are a "new creation," one whose life has been transformed into the lifestyle of a pilgrim who is on a quest to know and love God more profoundly. When you say, "I believe," it ought to mean something fuller, deeper, and richer in your thinking than those same words meant last year or last month or yesterday. The apostle Paul knew Christ as intimately as has any mortal. Do you know what his goal in life was? "That I may know him, and the power of his resurrection, and the fellowship of his sufferings, being made conformable unto his death; If by any means I might attain unto the resurrection of the dead" (Philippians 3:10–11).

Second, intellectual knowledge does not make "credo" belief, but real belief never exists without a factual foundation of knowledge.

A Baptist friend illustrated for me how superficially we often approach what we believe. A southern church met down at the river to baptize new members. One elderly woman was particularly excited about the experience, and when the pastor raised her up from the water she shouted, "I believe!"

Now this young pastor was nervous. He was officiating at his first baptism, so he was overjoyed by such enthusiasm. So he put her under the water again.

This time she shouted all the louder: "I believe!"

Wonderful, warm excitement swept through those gathered at the water's edge. Caught up in the emotion of the moment, the pastor lowered the lady under the water a third time.

"I BELIEVE!" she screamed.

"Now, sister Mabel," the pastor shouted, "I want you to tell us what you believe!"

"I BELIEVE this stinker's tryin' to drown me!"

A great many people are running around looking for something—anything—to get excited about. They want something to believe in, a central focus for life. But when you try to pin them down about exactly why they are so enthusiastic about some cause, their factual foundation seems thin and cracked, not much deeper than that of this water-logged believer.

Mind and heart *credo*

Two interesting tendencies exist side by side in our society. One is the opinion that a proposition must be "reasonable" before it deserves to be hung in the hall of truth. In other words, my mind is the measure of truth. Faith must be rational; it isn't truth if I can't comprehend it or analyze it in a laboratory. The other trend is to think it doesn't matter, really, what you believe, so long as you are sincere and emotionally committed in your beliefs. In other words, the measure of truth is emotion—the warm fuzzies of hope and comfort.

These two ideas are not logically compatible, but they have been blended in truly extraordinary ways.

For example, some people consider themselves far too sophisticated to believe in anything so ridiculous as a personal, holy, infinite God. Yet they feel most uncomfortable living without belief. Therefore, they customize their own *credo* foundation, building a sort of warm, cozy cabin from the logs of humanism, Eastern philosophy, and other self-actualizing affirmations. This cabin nestles safely away, deep in the woods of prideful doubt.

Others place their faith in the claims of science, proud to have overcome the old superstitions of the Bible. But still they believe the Bible has some value. It gives identity. Or the Bible "becomes" God's words as it causes some indefinable, emotional "truth" to well up in the consciousness. Jesus may or may not have been a real person. It doesn't really matter, for he "becomes" God to me as I follow his example and live for others.

As I write, the memory is still fresh of the disaster in Waco, Texas, in which members of the Branch Davidian sect burned to death. The fire that took their lives ignited when law enforcement officers invaded their fortress compound. But just as tragic are the untold numbers of lives shattered by cultists of various persuasions. We are invited to sample from a veritable smorgasbord of messiahs and belief systems. Studies show that people who choose to give over their savings and their lives to bizarre cultic doctrines tend to be well-educated, highly intelligent, and creatively gifted. I wonder if this is true because such people reflect with more depth on the meaninglessness of their lives and become all the more starved for something in which to believe and to belong—someone who bids them reach for an emotion-fulfilling purpose beyond themselves.

I may offend some of you by suggesting that another outgrowth of these tendencies sometimes attaches to the popular statements: "I have no creed but Christ" or "I want a *relationship* with Jesus, not a *religion.*" You may say this with the caveat that you do believe certain things *about* Jesus quite strongly, and your relationship with Jesus truly assumes his friendship and lordship as God and Savior over your life. If that is the case you have a creed and a religion, whatever you may wish to call it, for your faith is founded on truth statements from Scripture. You may react against the word *creed* because creedal traditions sometimes come to supersede biblical authority. In that mistrust I fervently concur. And you react against the word *religion*, because "religious" people often replace true spirituality with dead orthodoxy. I share that dislike.

But a word of caution must be injected, because there are those who truly do reject creed and religion. Their objective is contentless faith, *love* for Christ that never journeys beyond emotional catharsis. They relate to a Jesus that I have difficulty recognizing in Scripture or personal experience. So please bear with me if I bring up creedal suppositions quite regularly. I use the term *creed* unashamedly to mean *a statement, subordinate to Scripture, of those things the Bible says are true.*

The journey of transforming truth

With those understandings binding us, I propose that we undertake together the quest to know and worship God better, or as Jesus said in John 4:23–24, to worship God "in spirit and in truth." This is a quest for transformation, because its aim is not simply to learn interesting, helpful facts about God, but to be forever transformed by God in how we think and live. For that reason I divide our journey into three books, cor-responding to three areas of transforming knowledge from a never-changing God.

This first book considers how we know God and why I have the temerity to say that what I believe about God *is truth,* and what the world believes is untrue, wrong-headed, sinful, unsatisfying, and deadly. We will strain our mental eyes to see the person of God. This has to do with *theology,* an unpopular subject in an era when feelings about God take precedence over knowl-edge of him. *Theology* means "the study of God," and I believe that people are transformed only as they study the God they love. We also need to evaluate the three types of relationship between human beings and their God: (1) as he created them to be; (2) as they became in rebellion to him; (3) as they can be in Jesus Christ.

This third relationship will be the subject of book 2. You may have memorized John 3:16: "For God so loved the world that he gave his only begotten Son, that whosoever believeth in him should not perish, but have everlasting life." There is a way—one way—to escape the traps of empty rationalism, humanism, and emo-tionalism. We call this way "good news," the gospel of salvation through the life, sacrificial death, and bod-ily resurrection of One who was God and man. Book 2 will look at parts of what John 3:16 means. It will seek to lift the veil from the most mysteriously magnificent plan of all eternity—God's plan of salvation. Theolo-gians call this study *soteriology.*

Philosopher Francis Schaeffer entitled one of his books on the Christian life, *How Should We Then Live?* That question is a good way to phrase the focus of part 3: If we are creatures of the sort of God that our God has revealed himself to be, how should we live? If we have been saved from utter despair and death by the sheer love and mercy of that God, and if we are commissioned by that God to be salt and light in a world that badly needs both, then how should we live? What kind of parents, children, spouses, neighbors, and citizens should we be? What is the shape of a God-centered life? If the world seems to be out-of-control, and if things seem to be a mess, what is the attitude that builds peace and joy for a child of God?

These and other questions covered in book 3 fall under what is sometimes called the study of Christian *ethics*.

Packing for the trip

As they prepare to go forth on a quest, pilgrims are well advised to pack light. They will not want to be burdened with excess baggage, but they must take essentials they will not be able to purchase along the way. This is especially wise advice on the pilgrimage we now undertake. The Epistle to the Hebrews reminds us of all the men and women who have taken this trip before and then relates in 12:1–2: "Wherefore seeing we also are compassed about with so great a cloud of witnesses, let us lay aside every weight, and the sin which doth so easily beset us, and let us run with patience the race that is set before us, Looking unto Jesus the author and finisher of our faith. . . . " For a Christian, the study of God, of salvation, and of living, is a study of what we can see with eyes fixed upon Jesus. Further, the only way to see what hinders and what sins entangle—the excess baggage of our past and present—is to look upon Jesus, rather than upon ourselves.

If we must plan to get rid of misconceived ideas and thoughts, the most important tool in our kit must be the Bible. One young maintenance man for a large hotel had the habit of keeping a Bible in his locker at work and pulling it out for a short study on his lunch break. This, of course, did not escape the notice of the fellow who shared his shift. Over time they became friends, and at last the co-worker could no longer hold back the question that had been growing in his mind.

"Do you have a problem reading things?" he asked one day.

"No, I don't think so. Why?"

"It's just that you've been here about eighteen months now, and you still haven't finished that book."

Paul told a young pastor named Timothy: "All scripture is given by inspiration of God, and is profitable for doctrine, for reproof, for correction, for instruction in righteousness: That the man of God may be perfect, thoroughly furnished unto all good works" (2 Timothy 3:16–17). Those seem good reasons never to finish reading this particular book. It contains God's breathed-out truth. Its presence on this trip is of vital importance.

Finally, we will take some written creedal and confessional statements with us, not because they add anything to the Bible, but because they explain what Scripture teaches. I particularly will organize my thoughts around one set of statements, the *Westminster Confession of Faith* and *Larger* and *Shorter* catechisms.

There are a few reasons I prefer this creedal statement. One obvious reason is that I am most familiar with it, and when I look at Scripture I find the same transforming truths its writers found during years of exacting study. A second reason is that the Westminster statements have figured prominently in the teachings of a wide cross-section of Protestant churches, particularly those in the Baptist and Presbyterian or Reformed traditions. If you are part of a Bible-believing church your tradition has strong creeds to look back on. Your church may not refer to those creeds often, but they stand as a part of a heritage you should understand. These confessions and catechisms are not mere historical curiosities. The Westminster documents are an especially helpful summary of what Scripture teaches, framed with care by Christian leaders who met together over a period of years to witness to the Bible. At some points you may interpret the Bible a bit differently than did those men. Such differences contribute to the various denominations across the land. But in every word these leaders mightily strived to pen nothing but what they saw the Bible teaching, and we would be hard-put to field a like number who approached them in godliness and sacrifice.

I also prefer to use the Westminster documents because they stress things about God, salvation, and our lives that we particularly need to hear at this point in history. Their birth was in 1640s England, at an uncertain, bloody time that was at least as tension-filled as our own day. People have not changed fundamentally since God breathed his truth through the human writers of the Bible, and we share most of our problems with those who gathered in London to write a confession for the ages, dedicated to the glory of God, the edification of the church, and the quest to know God.

*What is the chief end of man?
Man's chief end is to glorify God and to
enjoy him for ever.* [Westminster
Shorter Catechism, question 1]

1

Quest for Life

n the introduction I said that you and I will now undertake a quest. But think back on your life to this point. You can probably see signs that your quest began long ago—a quest for *Life—Life* with a capital *L*. Has anyone who has any understanding of life at all not begun that quest? Is there anyone who has looked up at the stars in a night sky, or down at the delicate features of a newborn baby's face and not wrestled with life's fundamental questions?

Who am I?
Where did I come from?
Why am I here?
How should I live?
Where am I going?

Those are quest questions, and if you have never wrestled with them, then apparently a brain has been wasted on you. If a person doesn't examine such questions as these, what is he or she living for at all?

Many years ago I came across the source of answers to those questions. Since then I have been testing out the answers in my own life, and I have seen the answers at work in the lives of others. They work. They are true. They come with the only real guarantee. It isn't a money-back guarantee, because the ultimate answers to life don't cost money. They cost your life.

Notice that I don't guarantee that *my* personal answers carry any great wisdom; these are not my answers. I would never have reasoned them out myself. They are a gift. Further, there are only two sets of answers to these questions, only two directions to take in the quest for life. One set of answers is true, and all others are false; one direction takes you somewhere worth going to; the rest go nowhere. Most people in this world are going diametrically in the wrong direction, the opposite direction from the way in which their true quest lies. That is very sad because they obviously will not find that which they seek. What is worse, the nowhere they are going toward does lead somewhere. It leads unerringly toward death.

> *There is a way which seemeth right unto a man, but the end thereof are the ways of death.* [Proverbs 14:12]

All of that sounds dogmatic, and the politically correct path Western culture now follows does not accept dogmatism about final verities. This came home forcefully in a recent news story about the appointment of a new district head for the churches of a mainline denomination. The district was in turmoil because the former bishop had presided over the marriage ceremony of two homosexual men. Such a furor was raised that he decided to step aside so that peace could be restored. A "moderate" with the reputation for wisdom and diplomacy was elevated to lead the troubled churches and was interviewed for a newspaper article.

Would he sanction practicing homosexuals in the pulpit of his churches? No, he would not, he told the reporter firmly. Neither would he participate in legitimizing a homosexual union. The church had made it clear that it was not ready for such boldness.

"But are you personally opposed to gays in the church?" the reporter followed up.

"Oh, no, not personally. I think we are making a big mistake by not embracing this lifestyle option. And I'm sure it won't be long until their lifestyle is considered as acceptable as any other."

This must have confused the reporter just a little. "But doesn't the Bible reject homosexuality as a Christian lifestyle?"

"Well, yes. But you see, we have three guides as a church: the Bible, our traditions as a religious people, and the decisions our leaders make. The Bible is primary, but it doesn't have primacy."

This is the gist of the account of the interview, and I found that last statement fascinating. The new bishop has well stated the spirit of our age, though each person might fill in the blank with those documents or truth claims that are "primary" but have not "primacy." Authorities are handy things to have around: They give us pragmatic direction. They can help bind a people together. But, according to this leader, we must not take them too seriously. He chose three primary authorities he was willing to follow as long as it served the needs of church stability. What he believed to be true made little difference. No one right direction excluded all other ways—certainly not a direction based on the authority of a culturally-bound Bible that took such a narrow view of things.

The way that seems right . . .

To say that there is one single right direction, and all others are wrong, returns to the old Christian habit of proclaiming the existence of one exclusive truth. Wasn't that what caused the Crusades and the Inquisition? Isn't such a view unloving, prejudiced, and out-of-date?

Those are serious charges if it truly makes no difference which direction we take. But what if it does? The Bible quotation that begins this chapter is a proverb written nearly three thousand years ago by Solomon, a king of Israel. Old King Solomon makes a strong statement: "There is a way which seemeth right unto a man, but the end thereof are the ways of death" (Proverbs 14:12). I have cause for concern if Solomon is right, for he is saying that my inner compass is defective and needs to be recalled. What seems the proper course may not be. I am reminded of the fateful around-the-world flight of Amelia Earhart and navigator Frederick Noonan. In those days before satellites and tracking radar, Earhart's plane took off over the South Pacific and then disappeared forever. For decades, expedition after expedition searched for clues of where they went down and why. Finally some badly rusted wreckage was discovered on a tiny atoll, along with a boot like those the aviators wore. If this was, indeed, the site of the tragic end of Earhart and Noonan, they had drifted badly off course. One researcher reasoned that they may have become disoriented and changed their heading just slightly to follow a commercial radio signal toward what promised to be land and safety. If so, that signal became a siren song of death. It wouldn't have taken long over that trackless ocean to stray far off course. As soon as they missed their island markers they were doomed.

I fear for the churches led by such a leader as that bishop. He has a compass—Scripture—and he is checking it as one of the "primary" instruments he uses to chart the course. But he has secretly brought along a second compass of tradition and a third compass of current church politics. These can be relatively reliable, but only if they are constantly recalibrated to a reliable standard. For these compasses can be pulled off course by the radio signals of culture. The poor bishop may have enough trouble simply keeping an eye on these three compasses, but he has secretly sneaked aboard a fourth compass he didn't mention to the reporter. There is a way that seems right to him personally, a way that doesn't follow any of the other compasses. This compass is set to the way he personally wants to go. He is just waiting until the rest of us come around to his more all-inclusive truth. What is the authority that this compass is tuned to detect? The desires of God? I'm afraid he only listens for the tunes of his emotional feelings.

What seems right leads off in strange directions. We are warned by Solomon that the end of those directions is disaster. The stakes are high if Solomon is correct. What if there is one purpose for which you truly have been made, one and only one direction toward meaning in life, one and only one way to experience what life is all about? What if there is truth that leads to life and so is worth living and dying for?

Ultimate answers

Truths worth living and dying for: that was precisely what a group of Christians were called to Westminster Chapel in London to ponder just three and one-half centuries ago. The year was 1643—a moment of supreme national crisis. Theirs was no polite philosophical communing of theologians. England's Parliament had decided to tolerate no longer the despotic King Charles I. Parliament declared war on their own king and began raising an army under the crusty veteran Oliver Cromwell to face the king's army. It was Englishman against Englishman, and people were forced to take sides in a bloody civil war. How could Parliament justify such an act of treason, particularly since one of the most divisive issues that precipitated the conflict was the desire for religious freedom?

In one of their first acts as leaders of the rebellion, Parliament voted to call a conference, not of generals and statesmen, but of pastors. In effect their invitation read:

> Please come to London to help us! Study God's Word. Write a document that will bear witness if we are doing right or wrong! Tell the people what we are fighting for. Declare whether there is truth by which we must live and for which we are willing to die!

Between 1643 and 1648 these men, some of the most astute and pious Christians the church has known, met as the "Westminster Assembly": 121 ministers, ten members of the House of Lords, twenty members of the House of Commons, and eight advisors from the Church of Scotland. They were fallible men who sometimes argued passionately among themselves. But each day they devoted part of their time to listening to the proclamation of the Word, part of their time to prayer, and part of their time to deliberation.

In the end they forged three remarkable statements that came to be known as the *Westminster Confession of Faith*, the *Larger Catechism* (originally written for Christian ministers to memorize), and the *Shorter Cat-*

echism (for laypeople to memorize). The English Parliament eventually won the war but lost the peace, for
their own abilities to govern didn't live up to their con-
victions. Soon another king was on the throne, their
noble experiment to found a theocratic commonwealth
a dismal failure. Christians learned the valuable lesson that they need more than a political agenda or
godly leaders in power to transform a culture. But they
left us those Westminster documents as seeds that can
transform people.

There are other worthy statements of Christian faith,
and to be sure not every Christian agrees with all that
is contained in these writings. But on most matters considered by the *Westminster Confession* and catechisms
we can glory in our unity. We must do so, for these are
the central foundation stones on which our hope and
our message must stand. Here are ultimate answers
worth living and dying for. Let us look at some quest
questions, and parts of the *Westminster Confession* that
were written from Scripture to answer them. In order,
those questions and answers are:

> *How can I know any ultimate truth for certain?*
> "Of the Holy Scripture"
>
> *Is there a Source of ultimate truth?*
> "Of God, and of the Holy Trinity"
>
> *Is anyone in control out there?*
> "Of God's Eternal Decrees"
> "Of Creation"
> "Of Providence"
>
> *If there is a good God, why . . . ?*
> "Of the Fall of Man, of Sin, and of the Punishment
>   Thereof"
>
> *Is there any hope?*
> "Of God's Covenant with Man"

"Of Christ the Mediator"
"Of Free Will"
"Of Effectual Calling"
"Of Justification"
"Of Adoption"
"Of Sanctification"
"Of Saving Faith"
"Of Repentance Unto Life"
"Of Good Works"
"Of the Perseverance of the Saints"
"Of the Assurance of Grace and Salvation"

Then how should I live?
"Of the Law of God"
"Of Christian Liberty, and Liberty of Conscience"
"Of Religious Worship and the Sabbath-Day"
"Of Lawful Oaths and Vows"

What is my relationship to others?
"Of the Civil Magistrate"
"Of Marriage and Divorce"
"Of the Church"
"Of the Communion of Saints"

How does God lead his people today?
"Of the Sacraments"
"Of Baptism"
"Of the Lord's Supper"
"Of Church Censures"
"Of Synods and Councils"

Where am I going?
"Of the State of Man after Death, and of the Resur-
    rection of the Dead"
"Of the Last Judgment"

In these three parts we will look at each of these
questions and examine the Bible's answers.

The search for significance

With that introductory explanation, look at the quotation that begins this chapter. Actually it is a question and an answer. The question begins the *Shorter Catechism*. It asks: *What is the chief end of man?*

Is there a reason why I exist? What is it all about? That is *the* question, the one everyone wants answered. The answer is stunning in its simplicity and dazzling in its profundity: *My most important purpose for existence is to give glory to God and to enjoy him—to serve and live in communing fellowship with him forever!* I believe that behind this answer stands every word of Scripture. Does life have significance? Do I have any significance? The creed's answer is most fascinating:

My chief purpose for being is "to glorify God and to enjoy him forever."

But wait a minute. This answer actually robs me of significance. I become nothing more than a slave to some grand Potentate in the great beyond. If I must continually give away importance to some God, how is that very enjoyable? Desiring to glorify and enjoy God is not the direction with which most people have aligned their compass. Whether they realize it or not, they have framed their own answer to that question:

My chief purpose is to glorify me and to be my own person.

But there are costs to a self-glorifying philosophy as well. For example, men and women refuse to give themselves fully to a marriage relationship. They fear the loss of importance and self-satisfaction and control over their destiny. But how much satisfaction do the lonely survivors of broken marriages and casual affairs possess? Television image to the contrary, are those who enjoy the whole hedonistic singles scene truly so free and happy? Talk with the woman being treated for post-abortion syndrome, or the young man with an HIV time bomb ticking silently in his body about the glories of the good time.

Even inside the churches of our land are many who would gladly enjoy God, but only if that means God can be counted on to give them all of their desires. Unfortunately—or rather fortunately indeed—that isn't what our spiritual fathers saw in their Bibles. No, the men at Westminster found a far superior principle at work.

The blessing of open hands

Once upon a time, longer ago than I might care to admit, I was a newlywed husband charged in my marriage vows to give of myself fully, completely, and without reservation to the young woman I had married. Giving away of self didn't come easily. But ever so slowly, and after many mistakes, I came to realize that my enjoyment of the moments spent with this person I loved became more precious as I came to her with my hands outstretched and open, clutching nothing for self. There seemed to be an exact correlation: The more freely I gave of myself, the more I received for myself. What I demanded for self turned out to be no blessing at all; rather selfishness was a thief that stole from me the enjoyment that was freely mine.

The same thing is true when I come before my Father. When I live before him with my hands closed, grasping some area of my life that I don't want to share, life is neither enjoyable nor meaningful. But when I extend open hands and call him my Lord over some long-grasped tarnished treasure, the treasure is renewed and returned in a far more fulfilling form. Have I withheld time I should be spending in prayer? When I return to

God and give that time over to him, I come away
refreshed and fulfilled. For this is what I was created
to do. Do I withhold some possession, thinking that I
have given quite enough in other areas of life? I find it
becomes a meaningless toy that gives no pleasure.
When I extend it to the Lord, sometimes he blesses it
and gives it back to bless me. Or perhaps he takes it
away and gives some greater joy in its place. Am I sul-
lenly refusing to forgive someone, desiring mercy for
myself but justice for the one who has offended my dignity? I find my dignity is lowered far more by my anger
and pride than it ever was by what the other person
did to me. And when I open my hand and let go, I am
lifted and cleansed.

A passage that often is applied only to giving our
financial blessings to the Lord illustrates the blessing
of the open hand in all areas of life:

> He which soweth sparingly shall reap also sparingly;
> and he which soweth bountifully shall reap also boun-
> tifully. Every man according as he purposeth in his
> heart, so let him give; not grudgingly, or of necessity:
> for God loveth a cheerful giver. And God is able to make
> all grace abound toward you; that ye, always having
> all sufficiency in all things, may abound to every good
> work. [2 Corinthians 9:6–8]

The open, outstretched hand is a blessing because
we were made to give glory to God. First Corinthians
10:31 says that "whether therefore ye eat, or drink, or
whatsoever ye do, do all to the glory of God." The soul
shouts with the apostle Paul that "of him, and through
him, and to him, are all things: to whom be glory for
ever" (Romans 11:36). And what do we enjoy forever?
Will we suddenly become "healthy, wealthy, and wise"
because we have extended our open hands? One might

think so from hearing some statements that are made by those who promise prosperity for following Christ. God never promises that kind of blessing, and it might not be such a blessing if he gave it to us. Read 2 Corinthians 9:6–8 again. We will have all that we need to "abound to every good work." That may not seem like such a grand deal, but it is if we were made to glorify God and enjoy him forever. Paul is saying that we have all that we need to fulfil our greatest purpose for being. How many lottery winners can say that?

If you are a Christian and are feeling very unblessed in life every morning, great medicine awaits in Ephesians 1:3–14. Read through these verses with a paper and pencil in hand. Make a list of what is yours in Jesus Christ: gift upon gift upon gift, lavished on utterly undeserving rebels, now chosen, adopted as children of the Father, redeemed in Jesus Christ, and sealed by the Holy Spirit. Why? The last phrase of Ephesians 1:14 says the Christian is God's "purchased possession, unto the praise of his glory."

The two paths of faith

That sounds all well and good. But just as my early quest in marriage was full of trials and errors, so I often fail in my quest to give glory to God and to enjoy him. Loving God takes time and practice. I need help. Some of you who are married will suggest that your husband or wife has always been quite ready to point out needed improvements. As much as I hate to hear it, I need to know where improvement is most needed.

But where can I get the feedback I need to continue on in my quest for life with God? The *Westminster Shorter Catechism* makes the answer crystal clear:

> The Word of God, which is contained in the scriptures
> of the Old and New Testaments, is the only rule to direct
> us how we may glorify and enjoy him.

As we explore the Christian faith we will not be relying
on some 350-year-old confession. The men who first
wrote it would have been appalled at the very idea.
They wrote about what they saw revealed in God-
breathed explanations about himself and directions
for the quest. Alongside those fellow searchers we lace
up our hiking boots, pick up our backpack, and set
forth on the adventure of a lifetime—and more.

With all this in mind let us return to the ultimate
quest questions with which we began this chapter. I
am most happy to tell you that I have learned the
answers, and they are marvelous:

Who am I? I am a child of the King, a prince of the
realm (Romans 8:15–25).

Where did I come from? I came from the heart and
mind of the Almighty and Omnipotent and Omniscient God. I have been made a little lower than
the angels (Psalm 8).

Why am I here? I am here to serve and glorify the
Almighty and to enjoy him forever (Romans
12:1–2; Revelation 5:9–13).

How should I live? I should live according to the
commandments he has given to me in his Word,
which are designed for my good and my advance-
ment (Hebrews 12).

Where am I going? I am going to paradise, which is
beyond my comprehension, for "Eye hath not

seen, nor ear heard, neither have entered into the heart of man, the things which God hath prepared for them that love him" (1 Corinthians 2:9).

I mentioned that there are other directions beside the one the Bible recommends, and to be perfectly fair I should give a little time to the other side. A student who attends a college in Minnesota recently told me that his biology teacher said at the very beginning of a semester's class that his purpose was to show students that evolution is the way things happened and evolving species is the way things should be. He was going to do his very best to persuade Christians to abandon their faith and to adopt the faith of evolution.

That teacher is right about one thing: It is faith that we are talking about. You can't avoid making a faith choice when you set out on the life quest. The best known evolutionists have, for their part, often admitted that they walk "by faith and not by sight." Dr. L. Harrison Matthews, a noted evolutionist who wrote the introduction to the 1971 edition of Darwin's *Origin of the Species*, said:

> The fact of evolution is the backbone of biology, and biology is thus in the peculiar position of being a science founded on an unproved theory—is it then a science or faith? Belief in the theory of evolution is thus exactly parallel to belief in special creation—both are concepts which believers know to be true but neither, up to the present, has been capable of proof.

The evolutionist, the secularist, the person who rejects the direction in which we plan to quest has a very different set of answers to the quest questions. Bertrand Russell, one of this century's leading atheist philosophers, wrote a book entitled *Why I Am Not a*

Christian. In the book his answer to the ultimate questions of life was: "We started somewhere, we don't know where; we are here, we don't know why; we are going to some great oblivion, we know not whither."

That sounds rather depressing, to put it mildly. Others with a similar viewpoint abound. Here are but a few of their answers to the question, "Who am I?"

"A mere insect, an ant." (Richard Church)

"A fungus on the surface of one of the minor planets." (George du Maurier)

"A rope stretched over an abyss." (Friedrich Nietzsche)

"Small potatoes and few." (Rudyard Kipling)

"A jest, a dream, a show, bubble, air." (George Walter Thornbury)

"A hairless ape." (Arnold Schoenberg)

I would only add the comment of one more witness who has followed the other direction. "There is but one truly serious philosophical problem [in the twentieth century]," said the French author Albert Camus.

Only one? Only one question that you should be directing your mind toward? What is this singular problem at the pinnacle of the whole atheistic, evolutionary view of life?

Answered Camus, "It is suicide."

The danger of a blind quest

Against such profound despair, hear one more voice that calls all of humanity to turn to a new direction, toward a distant horizon: "For whosoever will save his life shall lose it; but whosoever shall lose his life for my sake and the gospel's, the same shall save it," Christ said (Mark 8:35). He was addressing, not only the despair of Albert Camus and the fatalism of Bertrand

Russell. He also calls to those who are frantically trying to save their lives by heaping up around them all comforts and pleasures, delights and securities, not realizing that everything they are doing is destroying the very thing they are trying to save.

The great eighteenth-century preacher George Whitefield spoke before most of England's nobility. One day the famous Lord Chesterfield came to hear him and became enthralled in a story he told.

A blind man left his house and with the help of his faithful dog and his iron-shod cane was making his way through the edge of a forest to the home of his daughter. He had made the trip hundreds of times. He knew it by heart.

Suddenly there was an explosion of fur. A rabbit sprang out of the underbrush and disappeared into the forest. The hound yielded to ancient instincts and sprang after him, in spite of the pleas of his master. The man called and called before he finally gave up. But by then he could no longer feel the familiar path beneath his feet. He had wandered away from the path. He tried to retrace his steps and finally came to familiar feeling ground. Everything felt right so he started out again. There would be no problem as he had many times found his way to his daughter's house.

Only he was not on the path at all but was making his way ever closer toward the edge of a precipice that dropped off two thousand feet to rocks below. The blind man drew closer and closer, tapping with his cane, until finally his cane slipped out of his hand and disappeared into the silence below.

Hearing nothing he supposed his cane had simply dropped into the grass. He bent over to find it but felt nothing. This must simply be a slight drop in the ground below him. He leaned forward again. Now his whole trunk and shoulders and head were over the edge. If suddenly sight could have been given to those sightless orbs, he would have beheld a spectacle that would have sent his head spinning, as he was looking straight down into two thousand feet of nothingness.

But he could not see that sight and so he continued feeling for his cane. Surely this decline was deeper than he surmised. He reached farther down. His heels left the ground! He teetered back and forth! He reached for the ground to brace himself lest he fall, but there was nothing in front to steady him. Suddenly, with his arms flailing in the air and a scream of terror issuing from his lips, the blind man hurtled headlong into the abyss that gaped before him!

By this time Lord Chesterfield was so engrossed in this story that he pictured the blind man hurtling downward and leaped to his feet, forgetting where he was.

"Great God, he's gone!" he cried.

There is a way which seemeth right. . . .

How can I know any ultimate truth for certain?

What rule hath God given to direct us how we may glorify and enjoy him? The Word of God, which is contained in the scriptures of the Old and New Testaments, is the only rule to direct us how we may glorify and enjoy him. [Westminster Shorter Catechism, question 2]

2

The Only Rule

When Coral Ridge Presbyterian Church first developed a radio ministry we searched for a name that would guide us in this splendid opportunity to tell others about Christ. We wanted to share how important we felt the message of the gospel to be in an individual's life. "Truths That Transform" became our radio and then our television banner. In the quest for life we are changed, and our lives transformed, only by truth—the truth of a never-changing God. The truth of God is living, vital, and transforming in a day of confusion and ignorance. At no time in history has it been more important that people be established in the truth of God's Word.

Jesus Christ said, "Sanctify [change or transform] them through thy truth: thy word is truth" (John 17:17).

One young woman told me she believed the Bible to be the Word of God, so I asked her, "What would you say to people who asked you to *prove* that the Bible is the Word of God? What would you tell them?"

She thought for a moment in silence. "I wouldn't know what to say to them," she admitted.

You who say you believe that the Bible is the Word of God: Is this conviction simply a wish? A blind leap in the dark? The quotation at the beginning of this chapter is from the *Westminster Shorter Catechism*. It comes right after the question and answer we looked at in chapter 1. The writers quickly anticipated the logical question that question 1 begs that we answer. Let us assume the ultimate purpose of each person is to glorify God and to enjoy him forever. Someone answers: "Hey, that is great! I'm going to run right out and sacrifice my first-born to God. What would give him more glory than that? No, better yet, I will assemble $100 million and build the world's largest church. Stained glass everywhere! That will give God glory. Or maybe what God needs is a more glorifying government. A couple of well-placed bombs in the capitol building should be a big step in that direction.

"No? None of those things is what God wants from me? Then you have been no help to me at all if you tell me what I should be doing, but you never tell me how." The men who wrote the *Shorter Catechism* were quick to lay the necessary ground—if there is *only one* rule to direct us how we may experience and reflect the

> *All scripture is given by inspiration of God, and is profitable for doctrine, for reproof, for correction, for instruction in righteousness: That the man of God may be perfect, thoroughly furnished unto all good works.*
> [2 Timothy 3:16–17]

glory and enjoyment of God, we had better know what it is.

The *Westminster Confession* relates:

> Although the light of nature, and the works of creation and providence, do so far manifest the goodness, wisdom, and power of God, as to leave men inexcusable, yet are they not sufficient to give that knowledge of God, and of his will, which is necessary unto salvation; therefore it pleased the Lord, at sundry times, and in divers manners, to reveal himself, and to declare that his will unto his church. . . .

The point made here is important. Creation shows God so clearly that not a single person who has reached the age of understanding will stand up before God and say, "I had no way to know you were out there." Yet salvation has not reached one person because nature displayed God before them. We will see later that the sin problem runs too deep. So God bent down to speak all that we need to know in words that we can understand, and that we can translate so others can hear and understand and be directed.

There is, however, a more basic question we must look at closely. How do we know the Bible is that "only rule"? Because 2 Timothy 3:16 and 2 Peter 1:19–21 and other passages tell us so? Why should we believe it? Many books are held out as true. Many claim that their truths are divinely inspired revelation. Why is this one different from theirs? How can I declare without a moment's hesitation that the Bible is the *only* rule of truth and is uniquely God's revelation?

Six facts, I am persuaded, conclusively prove that the Bible is God's Word to anyone who considers them thoroughly and objectively. In fact, those facts are so central to our Christian life and witness that if you get nothing more from this book than the fact that the

Shorter Catechism's answer is true, the effort will be worthwhile. If you approach the holy Scripture with confidence it will direct you to all other truth. That is, after all, why God gave it to us.

Here are those six facts:

1. The Bible stakes its own authority on its claim to be the Word of God. If it lies to us at this point it is altogether worthless.
2. The Bible at no point contradicts itself. Scripture is internally consistent.
3. The Bible's batting average for predicting future events—what we call prophecy—is 1.000. When Scripture says something will happen, it happens, though not always in the way we think.
4. The Bible's description of its contemporary world is accurate. Archeologists and historians have looked for that single finding that proves the historical data of Scripture to be inaccurate. In every single case where we have found the proofs, they vindicate the biblical content.
5. The Bible does not contradict the proven truths of science. No, the Bible is not a science book, but scientific findings agree with the fact statements that are in Scripture.
6. The Bible has been kept from error over history. Hundreds of hand-copied ancient manuscripts of Scripture have been uncovered. Some date back almost to the original documents. These manuscripts vary from one another in details. But not one of those differences in reading significantly alters a teaching.

The Bible's claims

The Bible explicitly and repeatedly claims to be the revelation from God Almighty to humankind. I would point out that most of the scriptures of various great religions make no such claims at all.

There is not the slightest hint in the writings of Confucius that they are a divine revelation. The ancient Japanese collected their tribal myths into the *Kojiki* and the *Nihongi*. These are the sacred writings of the Shinto religion, but no thinking Shintoist would call them divinely revealed. The sacred writings of Buddhism, Taoism, and Hinduism are "writings of the enlightened." The faithful believe that sages of old discerned these divine truths, not from a personal deity, but from the higher spheres of the universe. While Hindus disagree among themselves about the authority of the Vedic writings, few would regard them as direct revelation.

The Muslims' reverence for the Qur'an is complex and comes closest to our understanding of the Bible, but our conceptions still stand far apart. Muslims believe there is a divine book, directly written by Allah, but it is in heaven and quite unavailable to us. Allah revealed bits and pieces to human prophets, and the angel Gabriel gave God's "last word" directly to Muhammad, who wrote it down in much the way a secretary takes dictation. The *ultimate* Bible is in heaven, so the next best thing, the supreme authority to which Muslims look, is found only in the *Arabic words* of the Qur'an—the actual transcript of the dictation. An English-speaking Muslim who wants to read the true Qur'an must learn Arabic. The authority is in the words themselves more than the thoughts they convey, and orthodox Muslims scoff at the very idea of an English or French Qur'an.

By contrast, Christians look on the thoughts conveyed by the Bible as "inspired." Directed but not dictated by the Holy Spirit, people wrote in their own words, expressing through their own cultures and personalities, the truth content that God revealed to them: "Above all, you must understand that no prophecy of Scripture came about by the prophet's own interpretation. For prophecy never had its origin in the will of man, but men spoke from God as they were carried along by the Holy Spirit" (2 Peter 1:20–21 NIV). Paul tells Timothy that God has "breathed" or "inspired" all Scripture. For *that reason* it "is useful for teaching, rebuking, correcting and training in righteousness" (2 Timothy 3:16 NIV).

In his book *The Inspiration and Authority of the Bible*, theologian Benjamin B. Warfield offered the definition that: "Inspiration is that extraordinary, supernatural influence . . . exerted by the Holy Ghost on the writers of our Sacred Books, by which their words were rendered also the words of God, and, therefore, perfectly infallible." He goes on to make two explanations vital to our understanding: First, *the influence is different from the inspiration of a poet or novelist in literature.* A writer may win the Pulitzer Prize and still be in error. We may not totally understand a Scripture. We may misunderstand. We may take it literally when it is speaking in metaphor. But when we hear it properly it is infallibly true. Second, *the influence acts upon human beings who are expressing as they write their own emotions, language, and culture.* The words are those of people. Yet extraordinarily, supernaturally, the Holy Spirit guides those thoughts, ideas, and language so that they express God's direct revelation to all people at all places and times. I can say without apology that the Epistle to the Ephesians was written by a man named Paul and that its words are the very words of God.

More than 2000 times the Old Testament alone demands attention with the words: "Thus says the LORD . . . then the word of the LORD came unto Jere-

miah the prophet. . . . " Jesus stood before his followers and said, "I speak just what the Father has taught
me." These are utterly unique and fantastic claims.
More than that, I can stand as a preacher before a congregation and read out of my English Bible and say,
"Thus says the LORD," for the Bible claims to speak
God's thoughts to all, regardless of time or nationality
or language.

Making a claim and substantiating it are two
entirely different matters. But if the claim were not
even made then some would no doubt say, "The Christians are claiming for the Bible that which it never
claims for itself, namely, that it is a revelation from
God." Bible scholar and teacher J. I. Packer observes
in his book *Knowing God*: "Two facts about the Triune Jehovah are assumed, if not actually stated, in
every single biblical passage. The first is that He is
king—absolute monarch of the universe, ordering all
its affairs, working out His will in all that happens
within it. The second fact is that He *speaks*—uttering
words that express His will in order to cause it to be
done."

Contradictions and errors?

"Everyone knows the Bible is full of contradictions and
errors."

When I hear that I simply pull the New Testament
out of my coat pocket and say, "That is very interesting. I've been studying the Bible for years, and I haven't
been able to find one. Would you be so kind as to show
me where they are?" I'm still waiting to be shown. No,
the Bible is not full of contradictions and errors, and
those who say so have usually not read it even once.

We might remind them that A. T. Robinson, whose massive work entitled *Greek Grammar in Light of Historical Research* is the greatest work on Greek grammar that has ever been written, believed in the absolute infallibility of the Scriptures. Dr. Robert Dick Wilson of Princeton, who knew forty-six languages and was perhaps the greatest linguist who ever lived, was convinced that the Old Testament is absolutely trustworthy. W. F. Arndt and F. W. Gingrich, authors of the standard Greek lexicon that examines every word of Scripture and virtually all of ancient Greek literature, provide the most microscopic examination of the full meaning of the words in the Greek New Testament. Yet these scholars believed that the Bible is infallibly true and without contradiction. Arndt even wrote a book entitled *Does the Bible Contradict Itself?*, in which he looks at a number of supposed contradictions and shows that they are, indeed, not contradictions at all. The Bible is full of errors? The greatest skeptic minds have sought them. Their arguments, however, have failed and been forgotten, yet the Bible stands unscathed.

A window on the future

It is amusing, if very sad, to read the efforts to redate the writing of the books of the Old Testament. The object of this passion for changing dates is to argue that the stories are actually myths collected long centuries after the events they allegedly recount took place. One tactic is to look at the predictions made by the prophets. The reasoning runs: "Aha! Here is a prophecy in Isaiah that came true during the reign of King Nebuchadnezzar in Babylon. Therefore, this section is *obviously* post-exilic." Has it occurred to these scholars that God might have revealed to the prophets what would happen? Among some Bible scholars that possibility would not even make a hit-and-run appearance in their mind.

The people of the Old Testament world were not nearly so gullible as these scholars assume. In fact, they had in the law of Deuteronomy a simple test for proving whether a prophet had been sent from God: "When a prophet speaketh in the name of the LORD, if the thing follow not, nor come to pass, that is the thing which the LORD hath not spoken, but the prophet hath spoken it presumptuously: thou shalt not be afraid of him" (Deuteronomy 18:22). The penalty when such a prediction did not come true was death. That surely tended to discourage the making of predictions in the name of the Lord. And if the matter was taken so seriously, would writers be inclined to manufacture prophecies after the fact? There is much prejudice, but no proof, that the prophecies from God are anything other than what they say they are.

If that is true, then we have a rather strong authentication of Scripture. Again, this foretelling of the future in the name of the Lord is strikingly absent from all other religious writings. The writings of Buddha and Confucius offer no hint of prediction. The Qur'an prophesies only once, predicting that Muhammad would return to Mecca. This, of course, he proceeded to do—a rather unimpressive fulfillment of his own prediction. This is quite different from the prophecy of Christ, that he would rise from the dead. Literally hundreds of prophecies in the Scripture are concrete and stated with definite specifics.

In 1 Thessalonians 5:20–21 the Bible says, "Despise not prophesyings. Prove all things; hold fast that which is good." These verses deal with the two reactions to prophecy. One part deals with the contempt that has been instilled by our Enlightenment culture toward the idea that God would intrude in our affairs. The other reaction may very well reject Scripture, yet flips immediately to the daily horoscope in the newspaper or listens with rapt awe as a modern-day guru predicts next Thursday's apocalypse. Do people prophesy today? Jeane Dixon, we are told, has made amazing prophecies with astounding accuracy. I lack an overall box score, but during the 1950s she bravely prophesied all of the candidates of the major political parties and the winner in the national presidential elections in 1952, 1956, and 1960. We can safely assume she did not flip a coin, or she would have done better. Not one was correct. A vast leap separates the predictions of every modern soothsayer from the unfailing prophecies of Scripture. They have all come to pass as they were supposed to. Someone has counted 333 specific prophecies in the Old Testament concerning the Christ. Each of them was fulfilled in Jesus Christ.

Tyre

Almost every city and virtually every nation within a thousand miles of Israel were mentioned in biblical prophecy. Most of these are so definite that a high school student with an encyclopedia could check them, yet most people are not even aware that these prophecies exist. Take, for example, the cities of Tyre and Sidon, prominently mentioned by Isaiah and Ezekiel. Tyre was the capital of the world for 2000 years. It became to the sea what Babylon was to the land. Ezekiel uttered God's sentence against her in quite detailed language: "They shall destroy the walls of Tyrus, and break down her towers: I will also scrape her dust from her, and make her like the top of a rock. It shall be a place for the spreading of nets in the midst of the sea: for I have spoken it, saith the Lord GOD. . . . They shall make a spoil of thy riches, and make a prey of thy merchandise: and they shall break down thy walls, and destroy thy pleasant houses: and they shall lay thy stones and thy timber and thy dust in the midst of the water. . . . And I will make thee like the top of a rock: thou shalt be a place to spread nets upon; thou shalt be built no more: for I the LORD have spoken it" (Ezekiel 26:4–5, 12, 14).

So what happened? Nebuchadnezzar, the mighty monarch of Babylon, invaded the coastal regions and besieged Tyre for thirteen years before breaching the walls. The horses of Nebuchadnezzar rode into the streets of Tyre and the entire population was put to the sword. The city was sacked, a few of the towers were destroyed, a few holes were made in the walls, the city was burned, and Nebuchadnezzar returned to Babylon. Was the prophecy fulfilled? Certainly in part (Ezekiel 26:7). The city was destroyed. But there, jutting up into the horizon over the bleak Mediterranean, could be seen the remains of walls and mighty towers. Great piles of stones, timbers, and dust bore eloquent testimony that prophecies were not fulfilled. Who would come and take the huge stones and timbers of this city and dump them in the sea and even scrape the dust until this great mound of rubble would be a bare rock, a place for the spreading of nets? Who would guarantee that this city would be built and inhabited no more?

Ezekiel certainly did not prophesy this after the fact. A quarter of a millennium after Ezekiel died the prophecy had not yet been completely fulfilled. Then came a thrill of terror out of the north—a mighty conqueror clad in silver with armor of gold, plumed helmet, and astride his mighty horse Bucephalus. Alexander the Great appeared with the phalanxes of Macedonia and Greece. At Issus in 333 B.C. he dealt Darius III, the

monarch of Persia, the first crushing blow. Darius fled
to the east. Before Alexander followed him inland, however, he decided to nullify the force of the great Persian
navy by sealing off its seaports. The ports surrendered
quickly until Alexander reached Tyre. The new Tyre was
heavily fortified and built on an island, half a mile out
in the Mediterranean Sea. The Persians laughed at the
demand that they surrender. They felt impregnable in
their ocean fortress.

Alexander conceived one of the most brilliant
schemes in the history of warfare. He would build a
causeway across that one-half mile of water. Where
would such a vast amount of fill be found for this
undertaking? From the rubble of old Tyre, of course.

"Tear down those ancient towers!

"Destroy the walls!

"Cast the huge stones and the timbers into the sea!"

What had been the revelation of God to Ezekiel?
"They shall break down thy walls, and destroy thy
pleasant houses: and they shall lay thy stones and thy
timber and thy dust in the midst of the water" (Ezekiel
26:12).

I myself have seen pictures showing the nets of fish-
ermen spread on the rock of Tyre.

Sidon

Now compare the prophecies in Isaiah 23 and Jeremiah 27:3, 6 and 47:4 concerning Sidon, a few miles
north of Tyre. God said that famine and pestilence
would come, and he would send the sword. The city,
however, would continue (see Ezekiel 28:23). Sidon has
been sacked and pillaged many times, but it never has
been completely destroyed. It stands today. What do

you suppose our stand on the Scriptures would be today if Ezekiel had gotten his prophecies mixed up?

Samaria and Jerusalem

Jerusalem was the capital of the kingdom of Judah, and Samaria was capital of the kingdom of Israel. Concerning Jerusalem, God said he would destroy the city and tear down its mighty walls by the hand of Nebuchadnezzar (Jeremiah 24:9; 29:21; 35:17). But God also said that the walls would be built again, and the city would be reinhabited (Isaiah 4:3–6). Of course, we know all of that is true. The walls around the old city of Jerusalem stand today as an awesome sight; but what about the great walls of mighty Samaria, built high upon a mountain? Of those walls God said that he would cast down the rocks into the valley below, that he would destroy the city, that he would make it into a vineyard, and that he would uncover the foundations of that city (Micah 1:5–6). I have visited Samaria. Without even being aware of these particular prophecies, I remember looking over the cliff to see huge boulders that had once been city walls. Olive trees and vineyards were pointed out by our guide. Then I saw the great depths of excavations where all of the walls of other centuries, one dynasty after another, had been exposed. The very foundations of Samaria were laid bare.

Edom

These are but a few of the prophecies concerning cities. All of the cities of Edom were to be destroyed. The prophecies are striking and very specific. Jeremiah 49:17–18 says, "Edom [or Idumea as it was known in Roman times] shall be a desolation: every one that goeth by it shall be astonished, and shall hiss at all the plagues thereof. As in the overthrow of Sodom and Gomorrah and the neighbour cities thereof, saith the LORD, no man shall abide there, neither shall a son of man dwell in it." Ezekiel 35:3–4, 9 is more emphatic; the prophet declares that, because Edom (or Mount Seir, the mountain of Edom) had fought the Israelites in the time of their calamity, God would utterly destroy them. No one would ever build cities there again. Ezekiel 25:13 states, "I will stretch out mine hand upon Edom, and will cut off man and beast from it; and I will make it desolate from Teman; and they of Dedan shall fall by the sword."

These startling prophecies are exceedingly specific: No one would live in these cities; no son would be born in them. The cities shall never return. The extent of the desolation, both geographically and chronologically, is described. Here a bold gauntlet is thrown down before unbelievers. Have these spectacular prophecies come to pass? Listen to Constantin Volney, whose writings influenced Abraham Lincoln to skepticism in his early years. Volney visited Edom and saw the traces of many towns and villages, but "at present all this country is a desert" (*Volney's Travels*, vol. 2, p. 338). In Jeremiah 49:9–10 God declares that he would lay Edom bare. John L. Burckhardt (*Burckhardt's Travels in Syria*, p. 442) reported that the whole plain was "an expanse of shifting sands," and "the depth of sand precludes all vegetation of herbage." On Mount Seir the skeptic Burckhardt found only the ruined cities of Kalaab, Djirba, Eyl, Ferdakh, Anyk, Birel-Beytar, Shemakh, and Syk (*Travels in Syria*, pp. 443, 444).

Nineveh

As capital of the great Assyrian Empire, Nineveh conquered the world of its day, yet Nahum 1:8, 14 declares that "with an overrunning flood he will make an utter end" of Nineveh. "I will make thy grave; for thou art vile." All of the Book of Nahum prophesies doom for a city of idolatry and blood. Nineveh today is utterly gone. Nahum 1:8, 2:5–6, and 3:13 told that the Ninevites would flee in haste to the great defensive walls of their city, but the gates of the rivers would be opened and dissolve the palace. The gates of the land would be set wide open to the enemies and fire would devour the city.

The only detailed historical account of the fall of Nineveh is by Ctesias and is preserved in *Diodorus Siculus*. According to that account, Cyaxares, the Median monarch, aided by the Babylonians under Nabopolassar, laid siege to the city in vain. He was more than once repulsed and was obliged to take refuge in the mountains of the Zagros Range. Then, receiving reinforcements, he drove the Assyrian army back to the walls of the city. A blockade was unsuccessful for two years, until he received unexpected assistance from the flooding Tigris River. An extraordinarily swollen Tigris undermined the very walls of Nineveh, and the Medes entered through the breech. Saracus, the Assyrian ruler, burned himself in his own palace in despair. The city was laid waste, its monuments destroyed, and its inhabitants scattered or taken into captivity.

The total disappearance of Nineveh is confirmed by history. E. A. Rowell wrote that never had the world seen such a city. Its great rampart walls towered 200 feet, and on top chariots could race abreast. Gleaming in the sun, its lofty palaces and temple thrilled the traveler who was yet miles away. Yet in A.D. 627 the Byzantine emperor Heraclius fought a battle on the very site of the ancient city and was not even aware it was there. As recently as 1840 Bible critics assured the world that the city of Nineveh and its great Assyrian kings Sargon and Ashurbanipal were mythical. Little did these writers realize that their very words were confirming Scripture. Nahum 1:14 had warned the Ninevites that no descendants would bear their name. Nahum compared the men on the city walls to swarms of locusts that would disappear in the heat of the sun (3:17). Knowing all that we do today about Nineveh, it seems humorous. When a brick was discovered near the Tigris in 1840, bearing the name of Sargon, experts at the Paris Museum declared it a fraud. It had to be, since Sargon and Nineveh were just products of ancient imagination. Unfortunately for the experts, one of the earliest scientific archeological digs in 1845 uncovered the palace, the library, and finally the whole city.

Babylon

Babylon was probably the greatest city of the ancient world. Here was the magnificent temple of Belus and the wondrous hanging gardens. Babylonians invented an alphabet and developed a system of mathematics. They invented implements for measuring time and engineered enormous structures built from clay, the poorest of all building materials. They discovered the art of polishing, boring, and engraving gems, studied the motions of the heavenly bodies, conceived of grammar as a science, elaborated a system of law, and saw the value of an exact chronology. In almost every branch of science Babylon made a beginning. Much of the art and learning of Greece was born in Babylonia.

More than 100 Bible prophecies concern this city and empire. They cannot have been written after the event, because many of the details of the prophecy were not fulfilled until centuries after the Septuagint translation of the Hebrew Old Testament into Greek in 150

B.C. They cannot be said not to have been fulfilled. The facts are too well known. It cannot be said that they are simply lucky guesses. They have been minutely fulfilled. Nor can anyone claim that such events were likely to take place. Some were so incredible that, although history confirms them, we still stagger at the audacity of the prophets' boldness.

Herodotus tells us that the walls of Babylon had towers that extended above the 200-foot walls to a height of 300 feet. The triple walls of Babylon were 187 feet thick at their base, the mightiest ever built around any city. It is concerning the futility of these fantastic defenses that God says in Jeremiah 51:26, 58: "They shall not take of thee a stone for a corner, nor a stone for foundations; but thou shalt be desolate for ever. . . . The broad walls of Babylon shall be utterly broken, and her high gates shall be burned with fire; and the people shall labour in vain, and the folk in the fire, and they shall be weary."

Jeremiah says: (1) the wall will be broken down; (2) the wall will be broken down utterly; (3) the wall will be broken down permanently.

The walls were not suddenly destroyed. The city was taken by stealth by the Medes and Persians, and the walls still existed when Alexander the Great died there in 323 B.C. Their ruins still jutted into the sky on the day Christ hung on the cross, a reminder that not all prophecies had been fulfilled. The walls stood even into the fourth century A.D. Then an astounding event took place. Emperor Julian, usually called "Julian the Apostate" because of his desire to rid the Roman Empire of Christianity, desired to do everything in his power to destroy belief in the Scriptures. While engaged in a war with the Persians near the remains of Babylon, Julian completely destroyed remnants of the old walls, lest they afford protection to a future Persian army. Had he known of the prophecy he was fulfilling, he might have rethought this great undertaking.

When Babylon was mistress of the world, containing within its mighty walls 196 square miles of the most magnificently developed city of all time, with beautiful parks, lakes, aqueducts, and hanging gardens, Jeremiah 50:13, 39 made this further prophecy: "Because of the wrath of the LORD it shall not be inhabited, but it shall be wholly desolate: every one that goeth by Babylon shall be astonished, and hiss at all her plagues. . . . The wild beasts of the desert with the wild beasts of the islands shall dwell there, and the owls shall dwell therein: and it shall be no more inhabited for ever; neither shall it be dwelt in from generation to generation."

Imagine the reaction if I made such a prophecy about London and expected to be taken seriously. I'm sure that is how the people of Babylon would have treated this crazy prophet had they heard his warning.

Archeologists have uncovered remains of twenty or thirty cities on this site, which was most excellently situated on the Euphrates. The location offered fine possibilities of commerce. Militarily it was almost invincible. Its fields were so fertile that Herodotus was afraid to describe what he had seen there, lest he be thought insane.

Yet a sixteenth-century travel account recorded that not one house was to be seen there (*Ray's Collection of Travels*, p. 234). In the twentieth century only ruins remained to be shown to tourists. Even when the government of Syria re-created a gate and some other features of the city, they did not do it on the site. Will a city ever be built there? Ruins composed, like Babylon, of heaps of rubbish are impregnated with niter and sterilize the soil. The very vastness of the building materials of the ancient city doom the earth so that no gardens, hanging or otherwise, can be established.

There are other amazingly specific details in this prophecy. Isaiah's prophecy predicts that "neither shall the Arabian pitch tent there; neither shall the shepherds make their fold there" (13:20). Travel accounts speak of the common belief through all the country that the tel of Babylon is inhabited by evil spirits, and there has traditionally been a great fear of the place, especially after dark.

Consider two specific, apparently contradictory, prophecies in Jeremiah 51:42–43:

1. "The sea is come up upon Babylon: she is covered with the multitude of the waves thereof."
2. "Her cities are a desolation, a dry land, and a wilderness, a land wherein no man dwelleth, neither doth any son of man pass thereby."

Is this just a prophetic mixed metaphor? Perhaps, but consider that the ancient city now lies on the flood plain of the Euphrates, and two months each year the ruins are inundated by the annual overflow. After the waters subside, the area returns to its normal state, a dry waste like other cities of ancient Chaldea.

These are only representative of specific prophecies relating to the city of Babylon. The wrath of the Lord was poured out upon this wicked ancient city because that was his purpose (Isaiah 48:12–15). One traveler to the ruins of Babylon many years ago, a Captain Mignan, summed up the feeling all should have as we consider the retribution foretold and accomplished at that place: "I cannot portray the overpowering sensation of reverential awe that possessed my mind while contemplating the event and magnitude of ruin and devastation on every side" (*Mignan's Travels,* p. 117).

Do you want to disprove the truth of Scripture? Simply rebuild Babylon. But I should warn you of one man who even drew up plans for a new city on the plain, and he had the authority and wealth of the world at his command. Alexander the Great planned a trade route by sea from Babylon to Egypt. Babylon would become the central headquarters for his world empire. He issued 600,000 rations to his soldiers to rebuild the city. Almost immediately he was struck with a fever, and within days he was dead. The ruins of Babylon stand in mute testimony: "We would have healed Babylon, but she is not healed: forsake her, and let us go every one into his own country: for her judgment reacheth unto heaven, and is lifted up even to the skies" (Jeremiah 51:9).

"Scripture cannot be broken"

One needs only to read through the archeological journals of the last twenty years or so to see a continuing succession of testimonies. As political conditions in the Middle East allow excavations, the weight of evidence will only pile higher. If I wished to doubt, I would get no help from historical, archeological, and textual evidences. As this is written the long wait to see the full texts of the Dead Sea scrolls seems to be ending. Some have said that in those scrolls higher critics will have new proof that the New Testament is dependent on traditions of a dying and resurrected teacher revered at Qumran. But as the scholars dig deeper into the newly released texts, that connection already grows more unlikely.

Critics will continue to make brave assumptions based on the latest source theories, but their evidence turns out to be vague presuppositions, based on the work of some past scholar, who based his work on a skeptic before him. My heart cries for generations of brilliant minds, some of whom have honestly thought they were serving God, whose entire life works have been based upon a delusion. But I feel more sorrow for generations who perish because all they hear from the pulpit is the delusion. That delusion is that somehow one can break open the Bible, push aside the super-natural, and find within some underlying truth. Those who believe such a lie should listen to Jesus when he declares that "the scripture cannot be broken" (John 10:35), and when he prays for his disciples that the Father will "sanctify them through thy truth: thy word is truth" (John 17:17).

The *Westminster Confession* goes on to say some-thing else in the chapter "Of the Holy Scripture" that we will look at more closely in chapter 3. I can read the Bible twenty-four hours a day, and I will only be an exhausted Bible reader. It won't change me and I won't really understand its rule for my life. Sin runs that deep. The *Confession* says: "Our full persuasion and assurance of the infallible truth, and divine authority thereof, is from the inward work of the Holy Spirit, bearing witness by and with the Word in our hearts." This is one reason scholars can spend a lifetime in the Word and never feel the sanctification that Jesus prayed for his people. Only the Holy Spirit can make that truth come alive.

Is there a Source of ultimate truth?

There is but one living and true God, who is infinite in being and perfection. . . . God hath all life, glory, goodness, blessedness, in and of himself; and is alone in and unto himself all-sufficient, not standing in need of any creatures which he hath made. . . . In the unity of the Godhead there be three persons, of one substance, power, and eternity: God the Father, God the Son, and God the Holy Ghost. [Westminster Confession of Faith, chapter 2]

3

A God Suppressed

*I*n the last chapter I mentioned some wonders of the ancient world. In St. Louis, Missouri, stands a truly spectacular wonder of the modern variety. It is called officially the "Gateway to the West," but most people know it as "the Arch." The world's largest humanly engineered monument, its shining steel frame looks down from a far greater height than the Eiffel Tower, which once held that distinction.

The story of the construction of the Arch is truly one of imagination, daring, and precision. Its foundations lie some sixty feet below the surface of the hill on which it stands overlooking the Mississippi River. Yet the design tolerance for the two bases laid on those foundations was one one-hundred-twenty-eighth of an inch. So critical were the specifications that if the measurements had been off even one one-hundredth of an inch, the two great towers would not have aligned at the top.

I am indebted to a young Puritan scholar and St. Louis minister, David Wynkoff, who not long ago died in a mountain climbing accident, for pointing out a striking analogy between the building of the Arch and the importance of the first two confessional subjects we are considering. Christian faith rests on two pillars: (1) our view of Scripture, and (2) our concept of God.

We can, perhaps, misinterpret some teaching. We can be wrong about our view of baptism or the gifts of the Spirit. We may disagree about how a church should be properly governed, what will happen at the end of history, or any of a number of issues that stir debate among Christians. We should seek to learn the truth about such things, but we can be in error and not go radically astray or lead others to spiritual ruin. But we dare not err or plant our feet in sand regarding the Bible and the person of God. If we do, our entire understanding of Christianity will lack strength or consistency. Our faith will end up looking like the anemic twin arches of a fast-food restaurant instead of a stable, magnificent tower of steel. We will never even know how to live, because ethical decisions are meaningless unless founded in the absolute standards of God's revelation and his person.

> *For the wrath of God is revealed from heaven against all ungodliness and unrighteousness of men, who hold the truth in unrighteousness; Because that which is known of God is manifest in them; for God hath shewed it unto them.*
> [Romans 1:18–19]

Isn't it interesting, Wynkoff continued, that over the centuries of Christian history two teachings continually have been twisted one way and then another?

Today the two doctrines face bitter attack from within and without Christendom: (1) the trustworthiness of Scripture, and (2) the person of God. At no other points do people seem to be so blind or so relentless to suppress truth.

I was having lunch with a young couple—a man and woman who were articulate, intelligent, sophisticated, urbane, and had delightful personalities. It was a pleasure to chat with them. We got around to the subject of religion, and I shared with them something of the gospel. They let it be clearly known that really "we just couldn't believe those sorts of things."

Actually they were quite involved in the New Age movement. After they rejected the good news of Christ, I shared with them some of the incomparable evidences for the Christian faith and for the resurrection of Jesus Christ. It was fascinating to watch with what facility they were able to invent—sometimes it seemed out of thin air—all sorts of extraneous and absurd objections.

In chapter 2, I presented only some of the evidences for the truth of Scripture. Yet if you have determined in your thinking that the Bible is only a human book that is full of myth and fable, neither those arguments nor any others will be compelling enough to change your mind. At most you now realize that some of your assumptions about the Bible are not as safe as you once thought. Be careful. Once you let in a little light, the darkness never seems quite comfortable again. If I made that young couple a little more queasy about their assumptions, that is fine with me, but uncertainty will not bring salvation. The mind is capable of producing an enormous prolixity of arguments to counter the truth of Christ. The fallen human mind has a stake in unbelief. In the case of this couple at least part of that stake was easy to identify, for they were living together "without benefit of matrimony." After all, the argument goes, what is a marriage certificate but a piece of paper? And if their belief system is correct then they can remain warm and safe in a snug little dwelling place of assumptions they have built around themselves. No real societal pressure stands in their way. In this brave new world of relative truth and morality, how can anyone—even the friendly preacher at their luncheon table—cast stones at their alternative lifestyle of free sexuality?

But this warm, cozy little cabin in the woods of doubt only remains safe so long as the wolf does not enter the door. If there is an absolute right and an absolute wrong that have been established by an absolutely just, holy, perfect, and all-powerful God, then the sanctuary of the warm, fuzzy, fireside feelings of relative truth is no protection. The claws of truth rip away all pretense that we can stand before the God we have spurned.

The darkened room

Am I overstating the dangerous wolf at the door? "The wrath of God is being revealed from heaven against all ungodliness and unrighteousness of men, who hold the truth in unrighteousness," Paul tells us in Romans 1:18. But wait . . . If there is a God, then he doesn't have cause to get too upset with me, does he? I would have been willing to believe if only he'd pulled back the sky or sent me a personal letter. That is Paul's very point. He does not say that human beings haven't had the truth thrust before us. He declares that each person has the truth but suppresses it.

As Paul continues in verses 19–20, "that which may be known of God is manifest in them; for God hath shewed it unto them. For the invisible things of him from the creation of the world are clearly seen, being understood by the things that are made, even his eternal power and Godhead; so that they are without excuse." Psalm 53:1 puts it bluntly: "The fool hath said in his heart, There is no God. Corrupt are they, and have done abominable iniquity: there is none that doeth good." There it is again. We all have a stake in not knowing God, because our ways are vile. It is to our sinful advantage not to know him.

I do not suggest that this decision is conscious. I doubt many people are as forthright as one young college student named Bob who was presented with the claims of Christ.

"I won't believe, because you can't prove what you say is true," came his challenge.

"Well, I'm not so sure that is your real problem. What if I can prove to you beyond any shadow of reasonable doubt that God exists?"

He mulled that over for a second. "I suppose then I would be forced to believe."

"No, not really. No evidence can *force* you to believe anything you have made up your mind to disbelieve. How about it? Are you prepared to really look at the evidence?"

"No, I'm not," Bob said, shaking his head.

Gone was the arrogant challenge of his specious arguments against the existence of God. He was looking at his suppression honestly now. Some years have passed since that conversation. Maybe Bob's moment of self-understanding was a sign that the Holy Spirit was working in his heart. However, the truth-suppressing power of the fallen intellect is indeed capable of enormously potent self-delusion.

How potent? We will look closely at all the effects visited on humankind by the great fall into sin. But before we can understand our society's attempt to sanitize the land of all God-consciousness and we can discern why God's self-revelation goes unheeded, we need to realize something that Romans 1 and the men who wrote the *Westminster Confession* make very clear. Romans 1:28 declares of the human plight that "as they did not like to retain God in their knowledge, God gave them over to a reprobate mind, to do those things which are not convenient [or ought not to be done]." Looking at this and other Scriptures, and just looking around at their violent society, the framers of the *Confession* concluded: "We are utterly indisposed, disabled, and made opposite to all good, and wholly inclined to all evil" (chapter 6). That doesn't mean humanity is as depraved as it could possibly become. It means that the mind of each person who lives without Christ lives in a darkened, shriveled world, blind to what is all around.

Turning on the light of creation

Paul says God doesn't need to pull back the sky to reveal himself. The sky itself reveals him. "The heavens declare the glory of God," cried King David in awe (Psalm 19:1–2), "and the firmament sheweth his handiwork. Day unto day uttereth speech, night unto night sheweth knowledge." This language has stupendous implications for modern sophisticated Westerners who confidently assert that science has disproved God.

Has science disproved God? James Reid's book *God, the Atom and the Universe* states:

> Science is preparing a surprise for mankind! At least it will be a surprise for those who are laboring under the misapprehension that science has undermined the

Bible. In fact, it may even shock some scientists, who may be startled to find that their newly uncovered fact, or accepted theory, prepares still another link in the chain of evidence that is showing that the facts of the universe support the statements of the Bible, including creation.

As a man of science, Reid endeavored, under the old classic Newtonian physics, to discover support for the Bible. He was unable to do so. But then the old classical physics gave way to the new quantum physics, the atomic theory. A whole new concept of the universe emerged. As Einstein's theory of relativity revealed the inner relationship of mass and energy, Reid suddenly found that the new discoverers of science were establishing the teachings of the Bible. Many years later this process continues, and its consequences are incalculable. It takes a great deal more faith today than in the time of Voltaire to fervently study science and remain secure in materialism—the view that nothing exists but matter—no soul, no spirit, no God.

Astronomy

"The heavens declare the glory of God." No branch of science looks at a larger portion of God's handiwork than do astronomers. Carl Sagan to the contrary, I have read that 90 percent of all astronomers today believe in God. Then a higher percentage of astronomers believe than of butchers, bakers, or candlestick makers.

At the same time as Voltaire and the French Revolution instituted France as the crowning jewel of skepticism, a Frenchman named Pierre-Simon Laplace was establishing the modern marriage of mathematics and astronomy. Laplace said that the proof in favor of an intelligent God as the Author of creation "stood as

infinity to unity against any other hypothesis of ultimate causation." No other explanation for both the
infinity and unity of the universe seems remotely plau-
sible. It was far more probable, he said, that a set of
writing implements thrown promiscuously against
parchment produced Homer's *Iliad* than that the cosmos originated by chance.

Of course astronomy has come far since Laplace's
work in the late 1700s and early 1800s. So let us listen
to one of the leaders of twentieth-century astronomy,
Sir James Hopwood Jeans. As he looked out into the
cosmos, Jeans said that the more he examined the vast
expanses of space and the tremendous complexity of
the universe, the more the universe seemed to be one
gigantic thought of a pure mathematician.

Those who represent the case for creation call this
the *cosmological argument*. It is persuasive, for it
applies Psalm 19 to the world of science. "The heavens
declare," David said. As Jeans and other astronomers
take into account the diversity, complexity, order,
beauty, and sheer mathematical precision of infinite
space, David's words in Psalm 19:2 seem all the more
true: Day after day they pour forth speech; night after
night they display knowledge. Quantum physics has
demonstrated that when you get down to the subatomic
particles there is an irresistible urge of electrons toward
symmetry. This same urge is repeated in the very formation of the galaxy and even in the way galaxies move
in relation to one another.

Earth science

The findings of astronomy seem so incomprehensi-
bly vast, that perhaps we should move closer to home.
The cosmological argument for the existence of God

applies here on spaceship earth as well, but let us move to another howl of the wolf lurking outside the cabin in the dark woods of doubt. This is the *teleological argument*. The word *telos* in Greek means the "end." Teleology is that view of philosophy that sees in the universe that things were designed for a purpose—an end. Evolutionists do not like the words *design*, *purpose*, and *teleology*. They believe it is all one gigantic accident, the combination of infinitely long time and chance. With the advances in science over recent decades, it requires a remarkable degree of faith (or suppression, Paul would say) to believe that.

Consider the mass and size of this planet. The gravitational field of objects of certain weight and density allows life to flourish, or even exist. The gravity of Jupiter would give all organic life the dimensions of a pancake. The moon's gravitational field works the tides on earth but is not sufficient to form a life-sustaining atmosphere on its own shores. It is only by taking most of what we need with us that we humans can visit the moon, and the problems of planting a colony there are staggering. Just how much tolerance does the size and mass of a planet allow for life to thrive? One scientist figures that if earth were 10 percent larger or 10 percent smaller, earth would be desolate.

The interplanetary probes have underscored the fact that we are at an unusually precise distance from the sun. We receive just the right amount of heat and light. Our planetary orbit takes us much closer to the sun at some times of the year than at others. If we veered much from this flight path we would become a toasted Venus or a frigid Mars. Temperatures on neither will support life as we can conceive of it. Combine this with the tilt of the axis of the earth. None of the other planets in our system is so tilted at 23 degrees. As the earth slowly turns, all parts of its surface receive the rays of the sun, much like a chicken roasting on a spit. Otherwise a portion would become unbearably hot, and a much greater portion of the top and bottom poles would accumulate masses of ice.

We have already mentioned the moon's pull on the oceans. God provided the moon as a maid service to clean up the oceans and shores of the continents. Without the tides created by the moon there would be too little water movement. Shores and coasts would become one stench pool of garbage. It would be impossible to live near them. Because of the tides we have continuous waves breaking upon the shores to aerate the oceans. This provides oxygen for plankton. Plankton is the foundation for the world food chain. Without it there would be no chain. Without plankton there would not be enough oxygen to create a living atmosphere.

There is the wonder of our atmosphere, a great envelope of 78 percent nitrogen, 21 percent oxygen, and 1 percent a dozen different trace elements. None of the other planets investigated have anything like this combination, and spectrographic studies of nearby areas of the galaxy show no sign of the necessary elements. In addition, the atmosphere's elements are not chemically combined, which would make them less usable, but they are mechanically mixed by the tidal effects of the moon on the atmosphere. The environmentalists make a point that the atmosphere is something we should steward. But it is not quite as fragile as they usually suggest, or we long ago would have choked in the carbon dioxide we dump into the atmosphere. Where does all this waste go? It is absorbed into the ocean—allowing animal and human life to continue.

Then there is the amazing nitrogen cycle. Nitrogen is extremely inert. If it were not we would all be poisoned as it combined with other elements. But, in fact, it is impossible to get it to combine naturally with other things. Nitrogen is definitely needed for plants, but how does God get the nitrogen out of the air and into the soil? Lightning continually charges the atmosphere somewhere on the planet, daily depositing thousands of tons of nitrogen to nourish the soil and allow plant life to continue.

Much has been said about the depletion of the ozone layer. This certainly is cause for concern, for this is a thin layer of the atmosphere. If compressed, the ozone in this layer would be only a quarter of an inch thick. Without it, however, life would not exist. Eight killer rays fall upon this planet continually from the sun, and without ozone we would be burned, blinded, and broiled. The ultraviolet rays come in two forms. The longer rays are deadly and are screened out by the ozone layer. Shorter ultraviolet rays are necessary for life, and the ozone layer lets them through. Furthermore, the most deadly of these rays are allowed through the ozone layer in just a very tiny amount, enough to kill the green algae. Otherwise algae would fill all the lakes, rivers, and oceans. Just think of it: We live on a tiny crust of earth, comparatively the thickness of an apple peel, bombarded from above by deadly radiation, while just beneath our feet lies an immense core of molten lava. We are suspended between burning from above and burning from below. I would be exceedingly nervous were not I confident that there is a competent Designer who holds me in the balance.

One more natural wonder must be visited before we leave our thoughts on the earth. That wonder is water. Little or no water has been found on our sister planets, though we now have a fairly good idea of their composition. Here water rules the planet. Water, the amazing solvent, dissolves almost everything except those things that are life-sustaining. In its ice form water breaks up rocks and produces soil. As snow it stores itself in the valleys. As rain it nourishes and cleanses. As vapor it moistens the arable land. It forms clouds in just the right amount. At any one moment just about 50 percent of the earth's surface is covered by clouds, filtering sunlight and producing rain. As steam it runs powerful machinery.

Other than bismuth, water is the only liquid that is heavier at 4 degrees above centigrade than it is at freezing. That may not seem such an important quality, but if it were not true, lakes would freeze from the bottom up instead of from the top down. All fish would die and all algae would be destroyed. Without algae there would not be oxygen, and we would perish. The earth continually pours out speech about the person and character of God.

Human physiology

Whitaker Chambers was an atheist and leader in the American Communist Party until he ended his own spiritual wanderings at the cross of Christ. What is interesting is that the turning point that roused Chambers from the cozy fireside in the cabin of unbelief was an ear. He was sitting at the kitchen table feeding his infant son. Like many a new, doting parent he was considering with wonder this miniature person who demanded so much attention. He casually meditated on the shape of the ear, so uniquely formed and perfectly designed to carry out its mission of detecting and channeling sound waves. Yes, designed. . . . There seemed no other word for it. Communism might have a master plan for shaping the world, but its designers lacked the power to shape a baby's ear.

Everywhere we look the body points to God. Our life is based upon the blood that flows in our veins. The amazing red blood cell, created in the bone marrow, immediately gives up its nucleus when it reaches the bloodstream. For any other cell, losing the nucleus means death, like cutting the heart right out of a person. But a red blood cell is formed like a donut with a thin membrane across the hole. Without its nucleus it is able to carry more oxygen for the body because of this membrane and its shape. Were it shaped like other cells our bodies would require nine times as many red blood cells to provide oxygen.

What gives ears and blood cells their shape and provides most of the extraordinarily exact information needed to create a living organism? It took science a long time to break even the most rudimentary secrets of life, the gene. We now have a new kind of applied scientist, the genetic biologist, who has learned how to effect the formation of this chain of amino acids that are part of every cell. In a vastly complex process, which geneticists are only beginning to understand, the genetic code duplicates itself in each cell of the organism, carrying the entire design for a unique individual. These chains must form in very precise order for life to be even remotely possible, yet no one knows why they form at all.

One mathematician with a sense of humor tried to run a computer simulation to calculate the statistical possibility of a genetic code sequence forming by pure chance. The best he could come up with was that the statistical probability is not one chance in 1 million or even in 1 trillion, but in 1 followed by enough zeros to roughly stretch from the earth to the moon. Since the genetic code was broken in the 1960s, being a materialistic evolutionist is about as logically reasonable as being a member of the flat-earth society. We pity the

poor soul who believes the earth is flat. We hire the evolutionist to teach our children.

How, for example, could anyone look at a human eye
and suppose that it just happened? Evolution operates
through the principle that nature provides what an
organism needs over the slow process of the survival
and reproduction of the more adaptive creatures. But
try to imagine what process of natural selection would
have adapted a set of nerves that could translate light
into electrical impulses that could be translated by a
brain. There are no half-way steps between no-eyes
and eyes. Nothing less than the fully developed article
can do the job. Yet what mindless force could begin the
process? For something without eyes the sun would
have been warmth. But what conceivable drive could
have needed to find a way to turn that energy into sight?
And having somehow found the need, what mindless-
ness evolved the focusing lens, the pupil that opens and
closes to control the amount passing through the lens?
Where did the clear, gelatinous material come from to
conduct light through the eyeball to tiny receptors?
And what of the nerve connectors that make the image
meaningful to the brain? But even this isn't the whole
problem. Having somehow developed the eye, nature
wasn't content, but universally created two eyes on a
horizontal plane, so that we not only can see but we
also have a range finder that determines distance and
perceives in three dimensions.

Did you ever wonder why tears continually flow
across your eye? To see clearly and comfortably the eye
must be continually washed with a secreted brine. The
superfluous brine is conveyed to the nose through a
perforation in the bone as large as a goose quill. When
once the fluid has entered the nose it spreads itself upon
the inside of the nostril and is evaporated by the current of warm air that passes over it through respira-

tion. It is easily perceived that the eye must want moisture. But could the need for an eye generate the simultaneous production of the gland that produces the tear and the hole through bone by which it is discharged?

This is the weakness of materialist theories for the origins of life. What we know about the abilities of a creature to adapt to its environment can account for superficial, simple changes. But as complexity rises, so does the evolutionist's need for credulity. To put the matter mildly, the belief that chance evolved sight requires faith presuppositions. Sir Charles Scott Sherrington, an English physiologist who wrote a classic work on the eyes, said, "Behind the intricate mechanism of the human eye lie breathtaking glimpses of a master plan." We have developed some fine cameras and telescopes, but the finest does not even vaguely approach the optical manipulation of light that the eye provides automatically. When the eye got ready to create itself it also had the forethought for its own protection, and built itself beneath the bony ridge of the brow. It even provided a nose on which to hang the glasses that some of us need and its own window shutters, the lids and lashes that bat dust out of the way and spread moisture. Evolution certainly thought of everything, if it thought.

Lastly we mention the incredible brain. Weighing but 3.3 pounds and containing 10 billion to 15 billion nerve ends, each a living unit in itself, it performs incredible feats. Evolutionist Sir Henry Fairfield Osborn said, "To my mind the human brain is the most marvelous and mysterious object in the whole universe." True enough, and creationist researcher Dr. Henry M. Morris holds that mystery up before all of his evolutionist colleagues when he says, "Therefore, men who reject or ignore God do so, not because science or reason requires them to, but purely and simply because they want to!" As Romans 1:28 puts it, "since they did not think it worthwhile to retain the knowledge of God, he gave them over to a depraved mind" (NIV).

Turning on the light

Let us return to my two young friends in the restaurant. Presented with all the evidence in the world, they will not move from the darkened room they have shut themselves into. They will not move by virtue of the facts alone to come to put their trust in any God, let alone the God of the Bible. One thing the Bible makes abundantly clear is that human beings with a stake in their self-centered lives are experts in fooling themselves. We suppress the facts. Materialistic evolutionists aren't the only ones who do it well. Suppose after reading the last two chapters this young man and woman say, "Yes, what you say does seem quite persuasive. It seems difficult to believe in evolution. But our philosophy still works for us. If God is big enough to do all you say, then he certainly isn't concerned about our little lives. And who knows what kind of spiritual life forces may actually be the unseen guides of the universe? Why, there are those who are able to connect into them. We can even merge into that life force and so become one with the God you are telling us about. We have faith."

Their explanation might proceed in any of a number of directions and never stir from the cozy cabin. The occupant need only paint the outside with the colors of a belief system that best fits current needs and desires. Many people are quite willing to accept the Bible on a strictly intellectual basis. Their suppression mechanism simply filters and colors the light so that it

no longer carries truth to their heart. After years of
study and more years in the study and pulpit, ministers by the thousands continue to deny that God or the
Bible has any meaning or gives any hope. I have known
a few who came to find true faith and new life in Christ
after they were in preaching or teaching ministry. "Why
didn't I see it?" they ask. "Such wondrous things were
right there all the time. I read about them. I knew about
them. But I never took them in." The darkened room
looks so gloomy and carries such an odor of death when
viewed from the light and life of God's truth.

Who or What is the Source of ultimate truth?

He is the alone foundation of all being, of whom, through whom, and to whom are all things; and hath made most sovereign dominion over them, to do by them, for them, or upon them whatsoever himself pleaseth.
[Westminster Confession of Faith, chapter 2]

4

God Who Grows

C S. Lewis takes us to the heart of Christian experience in his philosophical and logical defenses of the Christian faith, but he slipped some of his most profound insights into the pages of five fantasy stories called *The Chronicles of Narnia*.

The first of these stories, *The Lion, the Witch, and the Wardrobe*, retells in a fresh way the gospel message. Four children are magically transported from our everyday world to a world that seems to be controlled by a wicked witch but is actually ruled by Aslan, a great lion who represents Jesus, the Lion of Judah. As I contemplate the person of God, however, I am reminded of another of the Narnia books, entitled *Prince Caspian*. In this tale the children, Peter, Lucy, Susan, and Edmund, return to Narnia after only a short passing of earth time but many centuries of Narnian history. Lucy is the first one to encounter the lion she has come to love more than life:

> "Aslan, Aslan. Dear Aslan," sobbed Lucy. "At last."
>
> The great beast rolled over on his side so that Lucy fell, half sitting and half lying between his front paws. He bent forward and just touched her nose with his

tongue. His warm breath came all around her. She gazed up into the large wise face.

"Welcome, child," he said.

"Aslan," said Lucy, "You're bigger."

"That is because you are older, little one," answered he.

"Not because you are?"

"I am not. But every year you grow, you will find me bigger."

How God must enjoy seeing his children grow to see him become bigger. He is no more omnipotent today than when he called the universe into being by the power of his word. He is the Ancient of Days, God Almighty *El Shaddai*, God Most High *El Elyon*, and Sovereign Lord *Adonai Yahweh*. He is the Immortal God, the Invisible God, the Just and Mighty One, the *Alpha* and *Omega*, eternal and ever-present. Once he reached out and pulled me out of the pit of my sin and I saw him as all-sufficient Savior and Redeemer. But, like Lucy, I have grown older, and now I seem to look higher to gaze into

> *I have heard of thee by the hearing of the ear: but now mine eye seeth thee. Wherefore I abhor myself, and repent in dust and ashes.* [Job 42:5–6]

his face. The God I understand and love is still only a micro-version of the reality that is beyond my comprehension. But as I continue to grow, so does my perception of who I am and who he is. That was the experience of Lewis, and of Paul when he wrote in Philippians 3:10–11 of his desire that he might "know him, and the power of his resurrection, and the fellowship of his sufferings, being made conformable unto his death; If by any means I might attain unto the resurrection of the dead." That is the experience of every believer who is growing in his or her chief purpose for living, "to glorify God and to enjoy him forever." I can't imagine a more wasted life than one who has warmed a pew in the church building and has a Bible sitting uselessly on the shelf, but who has never grown older spiritually nor seen God grow.

Through the blast furnace of affliction, Job found his own righteous life in its true perspective in relation to God's size. When his own pretense of righteous living was laid out before him, he said in 42:5–6, that it was like he had only heard of God before. Now that he saw him, all he could do was repent. Isaiah was ushered into the presence of God and he cried out in Isaiah 6:5, "Woe to me! I am ruined!" (NIV).

The straightedge

John Calvin begins his *Institutes of the Christian Religion*, one of the most influential works in the history of Christianity, with this introduction: "Nearly all the wisdom we possess, that is to say, true and sound wisdom, consists of two parts: the knowledge of God and of ourselves." Calvin goes on to observe that it is impossible to truly know oneself without a knowledge of the God in whom we live and move and have our being (Acts 17:28). Our knowledge seems true and logical when we keep our eyes fastened steadfastly on the material things around us. But what happens when we take God into account? Calvin writes:

> Suppose we but once begin to raise our thoughts to God, and to ponder his nature, and how completely perfect are his righteousness, wisdom, and power—the straightedge to which we must be shaped. Then, what masquerading earlier as righteousness was pleasing in us will soon grow filthy in its consummate wickedness. What wonderfully impressed us under the name of wisdom will stink in its very foolishness. What wore the face of power will prove itself the most miserable wickedness. That is, what in us seems perfection itself corresponds ill to the purity of God.

More eloquent pens than mine have failed to communicate what by definition is beyond the scope of language to portray. Even the *Westminster Confession* and catechisms show signs of the struggle these pious, learned men experienced as they contemplated God. They ended up with a compilation of the language Scripture uses, a stringing together of verse after verse after verse after verse. They seem to have been unable to sum up all those attributes and descriptions. Then they came to the writing of the *Shorter Catechism* and the question "What is God?" Now they were stuck. This catechism was to sum up the essentials of faith in a form a child could understand. Long and hard these men discussed all that they knew God to be. It seemed to defy abbreviation. Finally they adjourned for a time of prayer that God might give them special wisdom.

The youngest of the delegates, a Scot named George Gillespie, had not yet seen his thirtieth year. He began to pray: "Oh, God. Thou art a Spirit, infinite, eternal, and unchangeable in thy wisdom, power, holiness, justice, goodness, and truth. . . . "

"Stop the prayer!" shouted a voice from the assembly. "God has answered us." And they wrote down those words, which come down to us as one of the most beautiful and scriptural definitions of the person of God ever written:

> *God is a Spirit, infinite, eternal, and unchangeable in his wisdom, power, holiness, justice, goodness, and truth.*

Most church historians say that story probably is not how it happened, but it does seem true to my experience that, when I try to reason out God, my mind is simply blown away the closer I come. But when I open my spiritual mind in prayer, and apply scriptural precepts with the eyes of faith, I grow older; God grows larger. I can, with Calvin, "begin to raise my thoughts to God, and to ponder his nature, and how completely perfect are his righteousness, wisdom, and power—the straightedge to which I must be shaped."

God is a Spirit

We acknowledge a mystery as soon as we open the first page of Scripture and read that "In the beginning God created the heaven and the earth" (Genesis 1:1). Among the first things Scripture teaches is that God is not from our neighborhood. He is not bound by laws of dimensionality and size and mass as is everything else we know. This is an uncomfortably foreign Being, beyond our control and escape. The *Confession* begins its description: "There is but one only living and true God, who is infinite in being and perfection, a most pure spirit, invisible, without body, parts, or passions,

immutable, immense, eternal, incomprehensible. . . . "
Where do they get such terms?

> Lo, he goeth by me, and I see him not: he passeth on
> also, but I perceive him not. [Job 9:11]

> Whither shall I go from thy spirit? or whither shall I
> flee from thy presence? If I ascend up into heaven, thou
> art there: if I make my bed in hell, behold, thou art
> there. [Psalm 139:7–8]

> No man hath seen God at any time; the only begotten
> Son, which is in the bosom of the Father, he hath
> declared him. [John 1:18]

> God is a Spirit: and they that worship him must wor-
> ship him in spirit and in truth. [John 4:24]

> Howbeit the most High dwelleth not in temples made
> with hands; as saith the prophet, Heaven is my throne,
> and earth is my footstool: what house will ye build me?
> saith the Lord: or what is the place of my rest? Hath
> not my hand made all these things? [Acts 7:48–50]

Theology, the study of God, uses the word *transcendent* to describe such characteristics. God transcends
the earth and heavens and my understanding. Yet every
time I stand beside a casket of someone I have known
I realize that there are spiritual beings besides God,
and we human beings are among them. Though the
materialistic evolutionist tries to tell me otherwise,
there is obviously something going on in my conscious
mind besides electrochemical activity. And when a person dies something departs that had been inside the
body. There is simply no one at home any longer in the
arms and legs and torso and head lying in state. We
may gather in the funeral home and observe the craft

of the embalmer and remark, "How natural she looks, as if she is there asleep." But this is no sleep. That body lies a ruined house, silent and uninhabited.

For the Christian that relationship of spirit to Spirit is the fantastic hope of our faith:

> For whosoever will save his life shall lose it; but whosoever shall lose his life for my sake and the gospel's, the same shall save it. For what shall it profit a man, if he shall gain the whole world, and lose his own soul? Or what shall a man give in exchange for his soul? [Mark 8:35–37]

> The Spirit itself beareth witness with our spirit, that we are the children of God. [Romans 8:16]

> For if we believe that Jesus died and rose again, even so them also which sleep in Jesus will God bring with him. [1 Thessalonians 4:14]

> Receiving the end of your faith, even the salvation of your souls. [1 Peter 1:9]

The Bible generally speaks of three types of beings in the spiritual sphere: (1) Human beings are spirit as well as flesh. (2) Angels are completely spirit, though they are also finite, even as we. That fact gives me considerable comfort when I think about the spiritual warfare that involves the holy angels, the angels in rebellion against God, and me. Angels are limited, too. (3) Then there is God, the infinite Spirit who is unbound, so that we are never outside his presence.

The *Confession* calls him a "most pure spirit." In the language of the 1640s the writers said that he is "without passions." The meaning of *passions* has changed somewhat over the intervening centuries. They were not saying that God is without emotions, and Scripture has much to say about God's emotions. In modern language the *Confession* means that God's emotions are never uncontrolled. Given how often my sin gives God cause for uncontrolled anger, I am most thankful that self-control is part of the innate character of his spirit.

In chapter 5 we will consider the Holy Spirit within God's nature as Trinity. I will share then why I am especially grateful for this particular aspect of God's spiritual self.

Infinite, eternal, unchangeable

Considerable nonsense masquerading as theological wisdom has centered in these descriptive terms.

Infinity

God is infinite. He must, then, be unreachable, it is said. He transcends all of the temporal, spatial universe; logically he cannot be imminently in touch with my life. What sanctified baloney. If God's transcendence meant he could not be imminently concerned with the world he would be a very limited God indeed, a Jolly Green Giant too big to help pick the peas. It may not seem reasonable that an infinitely present God would be concerned about this corner of his creation, but it is hardly possible that he would not be *able* to do so as he wills.

"Ah," says the skeptic. "When you speak of God's *will* you have reached the logical impossibility of an infinite God. Your theism has no answer for that old question: 'Can God create a stone so large that he cannot lift it?'" I doubt there are many people serious about talking to lost people who have not heard this trite cliché. The answer is simple. Of course God cannot do so, for if he did he would be acting against who he is as God. To say that God is infinite does not imply that there are no things outside of his ability. The Bible says that God cannot lie, nor go back on his promise (see Numbers 23:19–20; 1 Samuel 15:29); if Jesus had failed in his mission to be the sacrifice for sin, God would have ceased to be an infinite God. That is what God shows Abram in Genesis 15:8–21. Neither can God dwell in the presence of sin, nor anything that is imperfect or unholy. Otherwise Jesus would not have had to die. Could not God simply have invented another way to deal with the sin problem? He could not and have remained true to his infinite holiness. God cannot sin nor tempt others to sin (James 1:13). It was only when Jesus laid aside infinity for a season that he could inhabit an infant's body and could be tempted as the second Adam.

The Children's Catechism, a much more recent writing than the Westminster documents, was prepared as a first step toward understanding God. It is used by several denominations. This catechism sums up the answer to the above objections to God's infinity nicely. The question is, "Can God do anything?" The answer: "Yes, God can do *all his holy will*." God's infinity means he is utterly free: He can do anything that he wants.

Solomon declared the true meaning of infinity when he built a temple, not to box God into a piece of geography, but to demonstrate his boundlessness:

> But will God indeed dwell on the earth? behold, the heaven and heaven of heavens cannot contain thee; how much less this house that I have builded? Yet have thou respect upon the prayer of thy servant, and to his supplication, O LORD my God, to hearken unto the cry and

to the prayer, which thy servant prayeth before thee
today. [1 Kings 8:27–28; 2 Chronicles 6:18–19]

This is true infinity: to fill all and yet hearken to the
prayers offered by small voices in his presence.

Eternality

God is eternal. In his book and television miniseries
Cosmos, Carl Sagan says, "The cosmos is all there ever
was, all there is, and all there ever will be." That is his
statement of faith. As we have said, such statements
quite ignore the problem of the origin of matter. Some
materialists claim that matter and energy are eternal.
Certainly no true scientist could miss the problems that
theory implies for the laws of physics, but it is the best
answer available to solve the problem of the *first cause*.
Physicists accept the fact that somewhere there must
have been an "uncaused cause," the "unmoved mover,"
and that first cause cannot have ever been brought into
being. Something *must* be eternally existing. There
simply is no alternative. For the theist that first Cause
and Mover is God. Often the Old Testament saints confessed their praise to a God who is "from everlasting
to everlasting" (for example, Nehemiah 9:5). "'I am the
Alpha and the Omega . . . which is, and which was, and
which is to come, the Almighty" (Revelation 1:8; see
also vv. 17–18). The one who makes this last statement
is Jesus, the Christ.

Is God, then, totally outside the space-time contin-
uum, so that all times blend into one eternal now? I do
not believe so, though God certainly has perfect command and understanding of the future, as well as the
past. The Bible uses the metaphorical statement that
a thousand years are as a day in the time perspective
of God. That would seem to indicate a passage of suc-

ceeding moments, though one quite beyond our human perspective. God certainly relates to us in terms of past, present, and future.

Unchangeability

Another word you run across when listening to theological talk is *immutable*. Both words refer to God's utter constancy in being, will, and purpose. One twentieth-century heresy, process theology, claims that God is "in process of becoming." The god behind this statement turns out to be nothing more than a pantheistic being. Certainly the theologians who hold such an idea do not find it in creation or Scripture.

This does not mean the God revealed to us is stagnant. His governance of creation is exceedingly dynamic. Scripture has much to say about what this part of God does and does not mean. The following passages should give us an overview:

> The Strength of Israel will not lie nor repent: for he is not a man, that he should repent. [1 Samuel 15:29]

> The counsel of the LORD standeth for ever, the thoughts of his heart to all generations. [Psalm 33:11]

> But the mercy of the LORD is from everlasting to everlasting upon them that fear him, and his righteousness unto children's children. [Psalm 103:17]

> I know that, whatsoever God doeth, it shall be for ever: nothing can be put to it, nor any thing taken from it: and God doeth it, that men should fear before him. [Ecclesiastes 3:14]

> For I am the LORD, I change not; therefore ye sons of Jacob are not consumed. [Malachi 3:6]

Heaven and earth shall pass away, but my words shall not pass away. [Matthew 24:35]

Because God wanted to make the unchanging nature of his purpose very clear to the heirs of what was promised, he confirmed it with an oath. God did this so that, by two unchangeable things in which it is impossible for God to lie, we who have fled to take hold of the hope offered to us may be greatly encouraged. [Hebrews 6:17–18 NIV]

Every good gift and every perfect gift is from above, and cometh down from the Father of lights, with whom is no variableness, neither shadow of turning. [James 1:17]

One area of much argument concerns Scriptures that say God repented (or was grieved that he had done something). One place where God "changed his mind" occurs before the flood in Genesis 6:6: "And it repented the LORD that he had made man on the earth, and it grieved him at his heart." Another is God's statement to Nineveh through the prophet Jonah that he would destroy the city and his subsequent decision to spare it (Jonah 3:4, 10).

These two passages tell us something about God's character, but not that he is fickle. In the first instance we see the great decline into evil that humanity had plunged from the fellowship of righteousness God intended. He is shown to be a father whose child has run far into rebellion. The parent is grieved. This Parent was so grieved that his holiness demanded punishment and a new beginning. Yet that punishment also grieved him, so that he made a covenant with the race he had so nearly destroyed (Genesis 8:20–9:17). The clear testimony is not that God would have done things differently if he had had the chance to go back, but that he is touched by both sin and its results. He takes no pleasure in destroying the wicked (Ezekiel 18:23, 32).

The second example says much the same thing, with the difference that the judgment against Nineveh is canceled after the wicked people of the city became frightened enough to repent. Actually it wasn't canceled so much as postponed (see pp. 49–51). God had a lesson to teach Jonah and Israel. As wicked as the Gentiles were, God intended Israel to be a priesthood for the world. He knew he would not destroy Nineveh at this time; what is more, Jonah was pretty sure of it as well. But that did not make Nineveh's condemnation, nor Jonah's responsibility to them, any less real.

Infinite, eternal, unchangeable in wisdom

Infinity, eternality, and unchangeability are three lenses through which we can look at all things we can say about the characteristics or "attributes" of God. They are aggregate in six categories of the *Shorter Catechism*: (1) wisdom; (2) power; (3) holiness; (4) justice; (5) goodness, and (6) truth. These are not six separate pieces of God's being; rather, each of them is descriptive of the whole nature of God. God is all of these things always.

The wisdom of God is infinite. He has been infinitely wise from eternity past to eternity future. Theologians call this God's *omniscience*. That word is interesting, combining the words *omni* for "all" and *science* for "knowledge." All of our search for knowledge—our sciences—attempt to learn what God has known completely and fully. He is the source of the equation for the theory of relativity as well as the theorems of geometry and the concept that $2 + 2 = 4$. Omniscience means that God holds no false beliefs. The range of his knowledge is total, including all true propositions.

Theologians and philosophers worry much about the implications of omniscience. Does it mean that we have no free will because God's copy of the pages of the book of future history is already completely printed? Certainly the Bible speaks of God's knowledge of the future, and it also speaks of Jesus not being fully informed about the future during his time on earth. God chose to limit his own knowledge in that way. We also might deduce that God can know and take into account all possible contingencies of all possible actions. God's understanding would be total, yet each human would be able to do exactly what he or she wanted to do given the choices and limitations God had placed on that point of choice. We have little experience with omniscient beings to know how this works. We will return to this question in chapter 7.

This much we can say with supreme confidence: God's infinitely and eternally wise understandings and decisions have not and will not change.

Infinite, eternal, unchangeable in power

Alongside the infinity, eternality, and unchangeability of omniscience, God is revealed as being all powerful or *omnipotent*. As stated above (see pp. 83–85), God's freedom to act and respond is limited only by his character. He cannot do anything that would make him less than God. But he can do anything he wants and has been able to from eternity past and will be able to do so as the waves of eternity roll on.

In his book *The Concept of God*, Ron Nash mentions one of the more unusual problems that have puzzled philosophers through the years. If God is omnipotent, does that mean he can change the past? Or, to state it another way, if I hear that a plane has crashed, and I realize that my family was flying on this particular plane, is it wrong at that moment to pray that God has saved their lives? The event is over, so he already has or has not done so.

Whether it makes logical sense, I guarantee that this prayer will immediately burst forth from my heart, and bringing any concern to God is certainly not "wrong." Is it useless? Will God hear that prayer and answer it by putting the brakes on time and backing them up to change an event that has happened? Nash quotes Thomas Aquinas to the effect that God cannot cause an absolute contradiction. If I can say that something happened as a true proposition, and the past is changed so that this truth becomes untrue, we have a logical problem of the highest order. Nash prefers to say that God cannot do anything that would reverse cause and effect. That restriction has nothing to do with God's freedom or power.

Infinite, eternal, unchangeable in holiness

The infinite, eternal, and unchangeable holiness of God returns our thoughts to his transcendence or separateness (see p. 81). Surely we know that God is separate from sin. He is also separate and exalted above us and everything else in creation. The Hebrew word used to describe God's holiness carries with it the idea of "heaviness." Remember when young people showed they were impressed by something by saying, "That's heavy, man"? The ancient Hebrews had a similar idea:

> Who is like unto thee, O LORD, among the gods? who is like thee, glorious in holiness, fearful in praises, doing wonders? [Exodus 15:11]

There is none holy as the LORD: for there is none beside thee: neither is there any rock like our God. [1 Samuel 2:2]

And one cried unto another, and said, Holy, holy, holy, is the LORD of hosts: the whole earth is full of his glory. [Isaiah 6:3]

And the four beasts had each of them six wings about him; and they were full of eyes within: and they rest not day and night, saying, Holy, holy, holy, Lord God Almighty, which was, and is, and is to come. [Revelation 4:8]

From beginning to end, from Genesis to Revelation, nothing is more certain in the Bible than that God is heavy—and beyond our knowing. The Israelites had an object lesson about this holiness in the ark of the covenant, which was given to symbolize God's presence and law. The ark was kept in the Holy of Holies, the innermost part of the tent in which God was worshiped in the wilderness, and an inner room of the temple. The room was shaped as a perfect cube, symbolizing God's perfection, and a great curtain separated this awesome sanctuary from the people. Only the high priest could enter the Holy of Holies, and then only once each year, the Day of Atonement. And on this day the priest offered a sacrifice for his sin and the sin of the people so he would be pure enough to enter. He filled the holy place with a cloud of incense so that he might not look upon the golden cherubim above the ark. And with all this, the early priests wore bells on their clothing and a rope around their waists. They feared God might find the high priest's offering unacceptable and strike him dead. Imagine the other priests listening at the door. Would the bells continue tinkling?

Or would they be forced to pull on the rope to remove the dead body of one rejected?

Now remember that day when the lifeless body was that of the holy God himself, who defiled himself by taking on himself our sins. At his death on the cross the curtain that hung before the Holy of Holies to separate humans from God in the temple was ripped from top to bottom. That infinite holiness of God was now shared. The transcendent, "heavy" God has sanctified his people, so we may fellowship in his throne room.

Infinite, eternal, unchangeable in justice

Recently a well-known news figure was interviewed about his religious affiliation. His father, he said, was a very religious man, and he had learned at home to have a deep but private religion, whatever that means. But, he added, "My father did not believe that a good God would send people to hell, and I do not believe there is a hell, either." This man, and presumably his father, have joined the chorus of millions in adoring a God who is infinite in mercy but who is quite willing to let bygones be bygones. This is a gospel of cheap grace, a Christianity needing no Savior, no standard, no cross, no repentance, and no righteousness. By necessity this Christianity rejects both the Bible and Jesus, since both tell us quite plainly that hell exists because God is just: "Behold, all souls are mine; as the soul of the father, so also the soul of the son is mine: the soul that sinneth, it shall die" (Ezekiel 18:4).

Jesus said, "Shall not God avenge his own elect, which cry day and night unto him, though he bear long with them? I tell you that he will avenge them speedily. Nevertheless when the Son of man cometh, shall he find faith on the earth?" (Luke 18:7–8).

A man named Elihu, the wisest of Job's three friends, puts his finger on the questions we need to ask ourselves: "Shall even he that hateth right govern? and wilt thou condemn him that is most just? Is it fit to say to a king, Thou art wicked? and to princes, Ye are ungodly?" (Job 34:17–18). I know that no one hates justice—for the other guy. But it is, in fact, a condemnation of God to say that he offers only forgiveness and will take no action toward those who have rejected him and thumbed their noses at the laws he has made. Is not such a god a weak and despicable ruler? Elihu goes on to say that this is not the sort of God he believes in:

> Is he not the One who says to kings, "You are worthless,"
> and to nobles, "You are wicked,"
> who shows no partiality to princes
> and does not favor the rich over the poor,
> for they are all the work of his hands . . .
>
> God has no need to examine men further
> that they should come before him for judgment.
> Without inquiry he shatters the mighty
> and sets up others in their place.
> Because he takes note of their deeds,
> he overthrows them in the night and they are crushed.
> He punishes them for their wickedness
> where everyone can see them,
> because they turned from following him
> and had no regard for any of his ways.
> They caused the cry of the poor to come before him,
> so that he heard the cry of the needy. [Job 34:18–19, 23–28 NIV]

A loving god who is not just is not truly loving because he cares nothing for the oppression of the weak by the mighty, and he is not very holy, for he permissively lets people walk all over him. We would call such permissiveness bad parenting or bad governing in our own society, but we demand it of God who is infinite, eternal, and unchangeable. I preach about hell, not because I find the subject pleasant, but because Jesus took my hell on himself, and now no one needs to go there. The good news of the gospel is not that there is no hell, but that its power is broken.

God is so much better than permissive. He is merciful—so merciful that we do have a Savior, a standard, a cross, and a means of repentance and righteousness. "God presented him [Jesus] as a sacrifice of atonement, through faith in his blood. He did this to demonstrate his justice, because in his forbearance he had left the sins committed beforehand unpunished—he did it to demonstrate his justice at the present time, so as to be just and the one who justifies those who have faith in Jesus" (Romans 3:25–26 NIV).

Infinite, eternal, unchangeable in goodness

We praise excellence by calling it "good." Yet Jesus considered "goodness" truly applicable only to God. To ingratiate himself with Jesus, a man called him "good teacher." Jesus immediately challenged this conception of goodness: "There is good but one, that is, God" (Mark 10:18). Jesus *was* the "good teacher" in truth, and the man's big problem was that he did not realize the full truth in what he was saying. God is transcendently excellent in all that he is, the perfect standard for what goodness is. Comparatively, nothing and no one else excels.

God's excellence extends to creation (Genesis 1:31), his love (2 Chronicles 5:13; Psalms 100:5; 106), his blessings (Psalms 31:19; 145), his works (Psalm 52:9), his power to restore (Jeremiah 33:11), his protection of his people (Nahum 1:7), his grace to all (Matthew 5:45; Acts 14:17; James 1:17), his gifts (Matthew 7:11), and his special grace to those who love him (Romans 8:32; 2 Thessalonians 1:11; 2 Peter 1:3).

God is perfectly good in all that he is and does, and the wondrous thing is that he imparts that excellence in the creative expression that uniquely connects all humanity with his creative perfection. Think of some great classic novel by Hugo, a play by Ibsen, a symphony by Beethoven, a poem by Frost, a cantata by Bach, or a dance by Nureyev. Some of our greatest artists and performers and writers and musicians have lived in complete rebellion against God, yet their talents still testify to his excellence. Even the elegance of a pro basketball player soaring toward the goal and the controlled explosion of energy as the Olympic sprinter leaps forward from the blocks offer an out-of-focus photograph of the excellence that is in God perfectly, infinitely, eternally, and unchangeably.

Infinite, eternal, unchangeable in truth

It was one of the saddest questions ever posed, and the most important he would ever ask. He was a judge, and the man on trial before him had said that he was a King, who had come to "testify to the truth."

"What is truth?" asked Pilate.

In a world ruled by deception fostered by the father of lies, truth is a rare commodity. We cynically pride ourselves on not being taken in by the con. We don't know the voice expression with which Pilate asked his question, but I wonder if his tone was not wistful. There was so little truth in his own life, so little truth in those he knew, and he had ceased to look for it. Yet standing before him was not only a man who was telling the truth, but who was the very embodiment of truth. Jesus had told the disciples the answer to this riddle only hours before: "I am the way, the truth, and the life: no man cometh unto the Father, but by me" (John 14:6). All successful searches for truth end in the presence of Jesus Christ.

If God is the Source of all truth, and Jesus is truth, we never know God fully in himself as he is, not even when we arrive in heaven. The full scope of infinity will remain beyond our ken. But we can know God as he is as he reveals himself to us. We can know something of the truth that lies behind the words: "God is a Spirit, infinite, eternal, and unchangeable in his wisdom, power, holiness, justice, goodness, and truth." Here are the sources of truth:

"Howbeit when he, the Spirit of truth, is come, he will guide you into all truth" (John 16:13).

"Sanctify them through thy truth: thy word is truth" (John 17:17).

Who or What is the
Source of ultimate truth?

There is but one only living and true God. . . . In the unity of the Godhead there be three persons, of one substance, power, and eternity: God the Father, God the Son, and God the Holy Ghost. [Westminster Confession of Faith, chapter 2]

5

The Absurd Trinity

he Trinity is a mathematical absurdity. Anyone who has progressed beyond the first grade ought surely to know that one plus one plus one does not equal one." That quote comes from the literature of a certain cult, one of many who have mocked the very idea of a God who is triune. A woman in my church once chided me that I really shouldn't speak of Jesus as God, "because when Jesus was on earth, God was in heaven, don't you know?"

As a matter of fact, I did know that. I also have progressed far enough in my education to know that one plus one plus one does not equal one. Nor do I believe that God is a cherry pie cut into thirds—three pieces, one pie. It has been said that the doctrine of the Trinity is one of the greatest evidences that Christianity is not a humanly devised religion. No one in his or her right mind could have devised such a concept. I think there are better evidences than that, but it does make the point that we need to be clear about what we confess to be true and what we do not believe. Many errors have arisen in the church in attempts to logically understand God as the Father, Son, and Spirit. This was complicated by trying to explain that Jesus possesses two natures: one divine, one human.

By the year 451 so many problems had appeared that a church council at Chalcedon tried to write a creedal statement that covered all the bases. We might wonder if the Definition of Chalcedon did not overdo things just a little. Part of it reads thus:

> We teach with one voice that the Son [of God] and our Lord Jesus Christ is to be confessed as one and the same, that he is perfect in Godhead and perfect in manhood, very God and very man, of a reasonable soul and body consisting, consubstantial with the Father as touching his Godhead, and consubstantial with us as touching his manhood; made in all things like unto us, sin only excepted; begotten of his Father before the worlds according to his Godhead; but in these last days for us men and for our salvation born of the Virgin Mary, the Mother of God according to his manhood. This one and the same Jesus Christ, the only-begotten Son, must be confessed to be in two natures, unconfusedly, immutably, indivisibly, inseparably, and that without the distinction of natures being taken away by such union, but rather the peculiar property of each nature being preserved and being united in one Person and subsistence, not separated or divided into two persons, but one and the same Son and only-begotten, God the Word, our Lord Jesus. . . .

> *Hear, O Israel: The* LORD *our God is one* LORD: *and thou shalt love the* LORD *thy God with all thine heart, and with all thy soul, and with all thy might.* [Deuteronomy 6:4–5]

I hope what follows will be clearer regarding what we are *not* saying about God, what we *are* saying, and why we *must* say it.

What the Trinity is not

The Trinity is not like anything else

Some say the Trinity is like water, which may be liquid, solid, or gas. This contains some illustrative quality, since all three remain water. Another version of this is that the Trinity is like an egg, which consists of a shell, an egg white, and a yolk. Another is that God is like a person who fulfils different roles at the same time. I am a husband and a father; I am a pastor; I am a citizen and a voter. I am all of these things at the same time and I simply fulfil one role and then another. God is Creator; God is Redeemer; God is Comforter and Guide—isn't this what God is like?

Such analogies break down so quickly that they are more dangerous than they are helpful. One of the first heresies the church faced was Sabellianism or modalistic monarchianism. Its adherents taught that God created the world, then put down that role to assume human form. At the ascension he put down that role or form and became the Holy Spirit. It is like an actor who performs on stage, then runs behind the curtain, changes costumes, and assumes another persona. God is not a thespian, nor is he moving from role to role. Nor is he now vapor, now solid, now liquid, depending on the conditions of the moment. He is Father, Son, and Holy Spirit—fully and at the same time. God does this in perfect unity, while the three natures remain distinct and functionally separate.

You don't understand this? Neither do I. God is not *like* anything else. You will find no corollary in nature.

God is. God is who he is. We don't have any choice about what kind of God exists. He comes with the package of life, so to speak. He didn't have to create us, love us, reveal himself to us, die for us—do anything for us. And he doesn't have to fit our mind's ability to conceive of him. The fact that he does do all those things is serendipity, or rather mercy.

Fortunately, God uses illustrations to reveal himself to us. The concepts of Father, Son, and Holy Spirit are his words, and they reveal aspects of tri-unity. Jesus is not a son in the same sense as in a human family. But the picture of sonship tells us much about the relationship of the Father and Son. John Calvin described God's pictures to us as the kind of language we use with an infant. The little one does not understand language yet, so we make sounds for the infant to model in its very first efforts to talk. God describes himself with the metaphors of a Father, an Eagle, a Shepherd, a Rock, a King. These pictures are ideas we can understand. But when Moses asked God his name, the name given was "I AM THAT I AM" (Exodus 3:14). We must hear that bottom-line answer. God can use our categories of knowledge, just as we can use an infant's categories to begin teaching about the world. But the categories only go so far until they grow. At the end, God simply IS, as opposed to every other sort of god, who ISN'T. God IS WHO HE IS, whether we understand or not.

The Trinity is not other

There are three major distortions of the concept of God: *deism*, *pantheism*, and *polytheism*. The woman who advised me not to think of Jesus as God because God is in heaven, is close to the deist frame of reference. The word *deist* means one who believes in a god.

But deism is belief in a certain *kind* of being, one who is "other" to our experience. *Deism*, as opposed to *theism*, which is the Christian's view of God, is belief in the existence of a supreme being who is the ultimate source of reality, being, and values but who does not intervene in human affairs and is ultimately unknowable. This defines God as the great clock maker, who assembles the works, winds it up, then sits back and meditates while the clock ticks away on its own.

Deism was popular in the seventeenth and eighteenth centuries because it approached God from a rationalist, Enlightenment perspective. Voltaire and Jean Jacques Rousseau made France a deist nation and paved the way for the atheistic, human-rights-worshiping French Revolution. That bloody time in French history tells us something about deism: The deist god is so out of the picture that he is no God at all in a meaningful sense. It was a short hop from deism to atheism.

A similar progression occurred in German theology, with more long-term results. Immanuel Kant, the father of modern rationalist philosophy and theology, in 1781 wrote a book that rejected all the arguments for the existence of God. He saw that our knowledge of reality is colored by our senses and emotions. So he deduced that we do not know *any* reality beyond what we can learn through our senses. We must reject all metaphysical knowledge. Kant erred, not in his evaluation of the mind, but in his estimation of God's ability to talk baby talk with us. He thought God too big—too "other" than creation. In fact, Kant's god was small. It takes a big God to fill the universe with his presence and remain involved in one speck of planetary dust in a rather ordinary galaxy. The small god remains rather conveniently out of the way, unconcerned with human sin.

German deism immediately attacked the Bible. Scripture's revelation was the point at which their small god collided head-on with the true, infinite, three-in-one God. Two of Kant's contemporaries, Gotthold Ephraim Lessing and Hermann Samuel Reimarus, founded higher criticism of Scripture. They believed the ultimate judge of Scripture was empirical science and said that Scripture's history and truth could be studied to see whether it was true or false. To this add Kant's rejection of human ability to understand the supernatural. Suddenly the idea is born that, if science cannot test God, he cannot be real. That is not quite logical, but that deduction came to be made, alongside the conclusion that we can test Scripture through higher critical theories and find "truth" buried behind the superstitious, unbelievable, unknowable, supernatural parts.

The Trinity is not "the force"

The god of the Enlightenment West is unknowable and transcendently "other," but there also is a tendency to err in the other direction. This concept of god is called *pantheism*. This word comes from the Greek *pan*, meaning "all," and *theos*, meaning "god." It means *all is god*; the universe is god. The immanence of god is emphasized until there is no distinction at all between god and creation. This idea dates at least to the beginning of Hinduism and some forms of Buddhism. A number of Christian mystics have sought to become lost in some great universal pool of God. If deism replaces God with reason, pantheism replaces God with nonreason. God is eternal but impersonal, and reality is a temporary emanation or manifestation—a life force, if you will.

If that language sounds slightly familiar to fans of the *Star Wars* movies, Luke Skywalker's and Darth

Vader's universe represents classic pantheism. The good and bad sides of the force are equally "god," and Luke releases his potential as a "Jedi knight" only when he learns to leave behind rational thought and be guided totally by the extrasensory power within him. There is even a pint-sized guru, the mystic Yoda, who leads Luke toward oneness with the "force." Reincarnation in Hindu theology seeks to lose the individual's consciousness, desires, identity, and rationality in the force behind creation. The end comes with absorption into the cosmos. The New Age movement expresses the desire to become one with the infinite. Its forms pervade society—from astrology and horoscopes to transcendental meditation and imaging.

It pervades Christian society as well. Have you heard anyone say, "It doesn't really matter what you believe [rational, substantive faith] as long as you are sincere [emotionally] about it"? That may sound quite open-minded, but the logical end of such thinking may be seen in the following report by a participant in the 1970 World Council of Churches' "Dialogue Between Men of Living Faiths":

> The dialogue . . . introduced most of us to a new spirituality, an interfaith spirituality, which I mostly felt in common prayer: who actually led the prayer or meditation, a Christian, or a Muslim, or a Hindu, or a Buddhist, did not much matter, what actually was said during prayer was not all important, whether a Muslim would say "amen" after a Christian prayer mentioning sonship of Christ, was not the question, what we really became aware of was our common human situation before God and in God.
>
> We were thus led gradually into a new relation with God, with our own selves, and with others, and this new relation was perhaps to what entire human history was moving.

Pantheistic elements infected Christianity in reaction to Kant's elevation of the rational mind. Three men were crucial to this process. The first was David Hume, who generally agreed with Kant about the mind's inability to comprehend God. Hume, however, saw a continuing nonrational need to believe. In the modern vernacular Hume told us to "Go for it! Don't worry about explaining God. Just pick a faith and make a great leap into the dark, into emotional catharsis."

Hume was a philosopher, but his preference for a nonrational faith bore fruit in the "German idealism" Christianity of Friedrich Schleiermacher. Schleiermacher announced all doctrines and propositional truths of faith to be nonessential "husk" that could be stripped away to expose *inner truth*. He said, in effect, "I agree that however God exists is unknowable. God is too distant to affect human moral reasoning. Who cares? Religion is not really about knowing or doing. It is about feeling, about ecstasy. I can still have a subjective, emotional faith in something out there somewhere that I do not see. So I will leap off this cliff I am standing on, and my 'feeling of absolute dependence' assures me that something out there will catch me." Suddenly theologians were stumbling over themselves to remove the Trinity, the virgin birth, the resurrection, and all supernatural husk. Deism was replaced by idealism, liberalism, modernism, and a host of other isms. The deist other-god had been poured into a bake-it-yourself cake mix of pantheism.

The next major thinker in this train was Karl Barth, a pastor in Switzerland during World War I. Like many who followed liberal Christianity, he was thoroughly disillusioned by the war, for humankind was supposed to be evolving into something better. The horrors of

war showed that this was not the trend at all. Barth totally rejected the unaware deist-liberal god, proclaiming an infinite, transcendent, and sovereign God. That sounds good—certainly nothing like the imminent god of pantheism—but with Barth and his followers things are not always what they appear. Bear with me while I sort out a few central teachings of what is variously called Barthianism, neo-orthodoxy, dialectical theology, or crisis theology.

First, Barth taught a creation and a fall of humanity. But this fall did not occur in space and time as we know it. Did it happen in history? That is irrelevant. What matters is that the fall is a principal in all people in all times.

Second, whether or not this fall actually occurred historically, the human being is so totally fallen that he or she can have no point of contact with God. God is totally other and is unknowable. Does that sound familiar? It gets even more complicated, though.

Third, God has overcome this gulf between himself and humanity by incarnating himself in the Word. In some sense the infinite became finite. Barth's view of God is that, in a paradoxical and mystical way, God stopped being infinite and revealed himself to us as Jesus Christ. He was not God and Jesus at the same time. Whether there was a specific time in which God walked on earth and was nailed to the cross and rose again from the dead is, once more, irrelevant.

Fourth, the Bible *contains* God's Word; we can even say that it contains the incarnate Jesus Christ. God's Word has authority. But the Bible is totally a human document. How do we know what is and is not truth? Well, the Holy Spirit incarnates Christ in our heart in the Word. What may be God's Word for you may *not* be God's Word for me. The dialectic push-pull of my emotional response ultimately gives it meaning.

I hope I have given an adequate overview of neo-orthodox teaching. Since truth is relative, its expression varies. Barth worked hard to find an adequate God and leave the pantheistic camp of the liberals. Actually he did neither. The liberals said the fall and the incarnation did not occur in history. Barth said it does not matter to faith. The liberal god was totally absent from the universe and imminent in the emotions. Barth found God unreachable except through a paradox—a putting together of two truths that cannot coexist. Barth saw Jesus Christ as God, but as a God that does not exist in the same time and place as the Father and the Holy Spirit.

The American theologian J. Oliver Buswell once personally confronted Barth on these points:

> I referred to his *Dogmatics in Outline* and asked if his view of the Persons of the Trinity, as there expressed, was not Sabellianism [see our description of Sabellianism or modalism above].
> "Well, you could call it Sabellianism," he frankly replied. . . .
> I asked Professor Barth how he explained the prayers of Jesus and His sayings in which He spoke objectively of the Father and of the Spirit. His reply was to the effect that in speaking of the Deity the difference between subject and object completely disappears. I said, "Is that not then mysticism?" to which he replied, "Well, you could call it mysticism."

If I were to poll theological writers and teachers, asking what theologian has most influenced their understanding of God, the Trinity, and Scripture, a majority would name Barth. That is unfortunate. We may admire Barth's courage against Adolf Hitler in Germany and his attempt to stand against the atheist understanding of liberal theology, but the root of Barthianism is mired in the marsh of the unknowable God, a blind leap of faith, and a rationalist view of Scripture.

The Trinity is not three gods

The third major distortion of the idea of God is the concept of polytheism, which says there are many gods. At least polytheism is not one of our problems in Western Christianity and our view of God. Or is it? I would suggest a tendency even in this direction among Christians who see God as something less than all-powerful against Satan. Satan takes the form of God's peer, rather than a limited, controlled, created being. Perhaps you have heard such statements as: "God wants to heal you. He is just waiting for you to unlock his ability by doing this or by praying in this certain way." "I am being besieged by Satan, and I can't get free because I haven't had the right people praying for me." Nobody who says such things would dream of calling Satan an equal of God, but that is an unconscious implication of this small-god thinking.

I am not forgetting that Christians are accused of being polytheists because of the Trinity. Some cults avoid that charge by saying, "Is it not the truth that there is one God, the Father? That Son is just a created being? He is really an exalted man who was created at some point in time, and the Holy Spirit is simply an impersonal force. The Spirit is the active force of God." This actually is an ancient error called *Arianism*. A distinguishing mark of cults is that they deny the Trinity. The defense of the unity of God will never come from philosophy or rational arguments. It is spelled out firmly in Scripture. Without deep roots in the authority of Scripture and a biblical understanding of God as the Bible reveals, the church's protest that Christianity is monotheistic sounds ridiculous.

The Trinity in Scripture

The Old Testament

The Trinity is more fully revealed in the New Testament. In the Old Testament God continually countered the polytheism of other cultures by impressing on the Israelites his *oneness*. But there are shadows of the Trinity in the Old Testament as well.

From the very first verse of the Bible we suspect that something is up, because the plural and singular forms of the Hebrew word for God sometimes appear together. God is plural—and he is singular. Genesis 1:1 says, "In the beginning God created the heaven and the earth." The word used in Hebrew for "god" is *Elohim* (plural), not *El* (singular). It says: "In the beginning God[s] created the heaven and the earth." Genesis 1 then switches to the singular form until verses 26–27: "And God said, Let us make man in *our* image, after *our* likeness. . . . So God created man in his own image, in the image of God created he him; male and female created he them." Genesis 3:22: "And the LORD God said, Behold, the man is become as one of *us*, to know good and evil." Genesis 11:7: "Let *us* go down. . . . "

Higher critical scholars make all sorts of spurious claims about mixed authorship in those early chapters, but that doesn't account for Isaiah 6:8: "Also I heard the voice of the Lord saying, Whom shall *I* send? And who will go for *us*?"

Jesus, of course, doesn't manifest his godhood in the Old Testament, but the prophets had a great deal to say about the coming Messiah, including his deity. Here are just a few of the passages in which the inference that the coming Christ will be God is strong. Psalm 45:6–7 says in reference to the coming King, "Thy throne, O God, is for ever and ever. . . . therefore God, thy God, hath anointed thee with the oil of gladness above thy fellows." Jesus himself and the Book of Hebrews quote Psalm 110:1 as indicating Jesus' deity: "The LORD said unto my Lord, Sit thou at my right hand, until I make thine enemies thy footstool."

Isaiah is explicit. In 7:14 he says, "Therefore the Lord himself shall give you a sign; Behold, a virgin shall conceive, and bear a son, and shall call his name *Immanuel* [Hebrew for 'God with us']." In 9:6–7 Isaiah continues, "For unto us a child is born, unto us a son is given: and the government shall be upon his shoulder: and his name shall be called Wonderful, Counsellor, The mighty God, The everlasting Father, The Prince of Peace. Of the increase of his government and peace there shall be no end." Jeremiah is just as specific, using a name reserved for God in 23:5–6 to refer to Christ: "The days come, saith the LORD, that I will raise up unto David a righteous Branch, and a King shall reign and prosper, and shall execute judgment and justice in the earth. In his days Judah shall be saved, and Israel shall dwell safely: and this is the name whereby he shall be called, THE LORD OUR RIGHTEOUSNESS." There are other texts that state it clearly: The Messiah, King, and Redeemer of God's people is God. Jesus is God.

The Holy Spirit enters Scripture in a full way only after Jesus returned to the Father, but he actively worked in Old Testament times as well. This is true in 2 Samuel 23:2–3: "The Spirit of the LORD spake by me, and his word was in my tongue. The God of Israel said, the Rock of Israel spake to me. . . . " Look also at Numbers 11:17, 25; Psalm 104:30; Isaiah 63:10–11, and Zechariah 4:6.

Some Bible students speculate that the Trinity is referred to in Numbers 6:24–26 when the Lord's blessing is given three times and in Isaiah 6 when the creatures seen in Isaiah's vision of the throne room of God cry out: "Holy, holy, holy is the LORD of hosts."

The New Testament

It is always interesting to hear people say, "You Christians say Jesus is God, when he didn't even claim that title for himself." Bible scholar Walter Elwell, in his *Topical Analysis of the Bible*, notes about 200 passages in the Gospels in which Jesus claimed godhood, claimed the prerequisites of godhood, or taught with an authority only proper to God. Here are some of those texts:

And Jesus came and spake unto them, saying, All power is given unto me in heaven and in earth. [Matthew 28:18]

And he [Jesus] said unto her, Thy sins are forgiven. And they that sat at meat with him began to say within themselves, Who is this that forgiveth sins also? [Luke 7:48–49]

Also I [Jesus] say unto you, Whosoever shall confess me before men, him shall the Son of man also confess before the angels of God. [Luke 12:8]

Verily, verily, I say unto you, before Abraham was, I am. [John 8:58]

Why then do you accuse me of blasphemy because I said, I am God's Son? Do not believe me unless I do what my Father does. But if I do it, even though you do not believe me, believe the miracles, that you may know and understand that the Father is in me, and I in the Father. [John 10:36–38 NIV]

Jesus may have been a megalomaniac, a liar, and a blasphemer, but do not accuse him of making fainthearted claims. Nor did he alone make these claims: John 1:1 says, "In the beginning was the Word, and the Word was with God, and the Word was God." John's Gospel refers to Christ, the Word who "was made flesh, and dwelt among us" (John 1:14). The doubting disciple Thomas fell on his knees before the resurrected Christ, saying, "My Lord and my God" (John 20:28). The point of Hebrews 1 is that Jesus Christ is above the angels as God.

We read in the New Testament that the Holy Spirit also is God and that the Holy Spirit is a person with tasks and responsibilities. Here are some of those passages:

> For it is not ye that speak, but the Spirit of your Father which speaketh in you. [Matthew 10:20]

> But when the Comforter is come, whom I will send unto you from the Father, even the Spirit of truth, which proceedeth from the Father, he shall testify of me. [John 15:26]

> But Peter said, Ananias, why hath Satan filled thine heart to lie to the Holy Ghost. . . . Thou hast not lied unto men, but unto God. [Acts 5:3–4]

> Know ye not that ye are the temple of God, and that the Spirit of God dwelleth in you? [1 Corinthians 3:16]

> The Holy Ghost also is a witness to us. [Hebrews 10:15]

> For Christ also hath once suffered for sins, the just for the unjust, that he might bring us to God, being put to death in the flesh, but quickened by the Spirit. [1 Peter 3:18]

We also can find some passages where all three persons of the Trinity are in view; for example:

And Jesus, when he was baptized, went up straight-
way out of the water: and, lo, the heavens were opened
unto him, and he [the second person] saw the Spirit of
God [the third person] descending like a dove, and
lighting upon him: and lo a voice from heaven [the first
person], saying, This is my beloved Son, in whom I am
well pleased. [Matthew 3:16–17]

Go ye, . . . baptizing them in the name of the Father
[the first person], and of the Son [the second person],
and of the Holy Ghost [the third person]. [Matthew
28:19]

When the Comforter [the third person] is come, whom
I [Jesus, the second person] will send unto you from the
Father [the first person], even the Spirit of truth, which
proceedeth from the Father, he shall testify of me. [John
15:26]

Because ye are sons, God [the first person] hath sent
forth the Spirit [the third person] of his Son [the second person] into your hearts, crying, Abba, Father.
[Galatians 4:6]

Is it necessary to believe in the Trinity? Certainly if
we believe the Bible we must believe this body of evidence. Loraine Boettner has said that, apart from the
doctrine of the Trinity, "the Deity of Christ, the incarnation, the personality of the Holy Spirit, regeneration, justification, sanctification, the meaning of the
crucifixion, and the resurrection cannot be understood." Jesus said, "This is life eternal, that they might
know thee the only true God, and Jesus Christ, whom
thou hast sent" (John 17:3). This is eternal life, to know
the triune God. Unitarians and Muslims and others
worship someone else, a lone, solitary person who
exists alone from all eternity.

What the Trinity is and does

But how can God be three in one? In the Trinity the
Father penetrates the Son and the Spirit, and the Son
penetrates the Father and the Spirit. Jesus said, "I am
in the Father, and the Father in me" (John 14:11).
Whatever that exact composition, the fact that God is
a Trinity is a fantastic blessing to us, because the three
take to themselves different roles. The Father, Son, and
Holy Spirit take part in the total relationship the
believer has with God in Christ.

First, the Father takes to himself three tasks: (1) creation and governance of all things in creation; (2) elec-
tion of those who will be saved, and (3) authorship of
the plan of redemption. John 3:16 says that God the
Father loved the world and sent his only Son.

Second, the Son takes to himself the threefold task
of redemption: (1) laying aside his prerogatives as infinite God (but not godhood itself) to assume humanity
and live a perfectly holy life; (2) suffering and dying in
the place of those who deserved to die, and (3) rising
victorious from the dead to ascend to heaven and send
the Holy Spirit.

Third, the Holy Spirit (1) draws sinners to God,
(2) applies the holiness of Christ to believers and guides
us toward true holiness before God in what is called
sanctification, and (3) comforts us in sorrow and speaks
for us before the Father.

To know God is neither to figure him out rationally
nor to rely on mind-submersing emotional catharsis.
To strike the balance of faith I recommend that you
read the revelation the triune God has given and med-
itate on what you discover there about the work of
these three parts of the perfect oneness of God. All
three are available to us in prayer, and it helps me to
recognize by addressing each in prayer, remembering

what they have done. There are examples of prayer to all three in the New Testament. Worship, praise, and adore each member of the Trinity, separately and specifically.

Hear, O Israel, the Lord our God, the Lord is one. And within that one there is Father, Son, and Holy Spirit—three persons in one God, forever, amen!

Is anyone in control out there?

It pleased God the Father, Son, and Holy Ghost, for the manifestation of the glory of his eternal power, wisdom, and goodness, in the beginning to create or make of nothing the world, and all things therein, whether visible or invisible, in the space of six days, and all very good. After God had made all other creatures, he created man, male and female, with reasonable and immortal souls, endued with knowledge, righteousness, and true holiness, after his own image. [Westminster Confession of Faith, chapter 4]

6

The God Revolution

nyone who shares the gospel with men and women in the community, whether using the Coral Ridge "Evangelism Explosion" plan or some other approach, quickly learns something about worldviews. It doesn't take long when discussing spiritual things to discern another person's answers to the quest questions, even if that person would not know how to phrase those answers. How one answers the question heading this chapter, "Is anyone in control out there?" affects every thought more substantive than which shoe to put on first in the morning.

Many years ago a great revolution occurred. Two titanic theories—and only two—exist for explaining the origin of the universe and the meaning of the life inhabiting it, whether on this planet or any other that may turn out to be occupied. When the theory of evolution was introduced it was not that one scientific idea replaced another, nor even merely that one worldview replaced another worldview. A supernatural view with ultimate meaning was pushed aside by an entirely naturalistic set of assumptions. Thomas Huxley announced that there no longer was any room for the supernatural. His equally famous grandson, Sir Julian Huxley, said, "Operationally, God is beginning to resemble, not a

Ruler, but the last fading smile of a cosmic Cheshire cat."

A world without its God

I don't think I need to sell any thinking person, whatever he or she believes about God, on the fact that a revolution of monumental significance has altered the mental fabric of much of the world. More Christians have been martyred in the twentieth century for their faith than in all other centuries of the Christian era combined. More people have been killed in wars. In the most medically advanced and best fed and clothed parts of the world, children are starving to death for food or love in the midst of neglect and abuse. Life in the twentieth century has been as cheap and disposable as in the depths of the cruelest, most degraded societies of the past.

> *Prepare to meet thy God, O Israel. For, lo, he that formeth the mountains, and createth the wind, and declareth unto man what is his thought, that maketh the morning darkness, and treadeth upon the high places of the earth, The* LORD, *The God of hosts, is his name.*
> [Amos 4:12b–13]

Look at one ongoing example in our own enlightened part of the globe. In 1980, eight years after *Roe* v. *Wade* brought about abortion on demand, a study estimated that 113,000 abortions occurred in the second and third trimesters of pregnancy. By this stage of development few abortionists would seriously argue that the unborn child is a "cellular growth" in the woman's body. At the very latest a developing embryo feels pain and begins responding to his or her environment by the late third month. By the fifth month premature babies are routinely sustained outside the womb in incubators. I find it difficult to imagine that somewhere around 30 million lives have been destroyed through abortion in the United States alone since the fatal Supreme Court decision in January 1973. Those who favor "choice" have all sorts of reasons to justify the majority of those killings occurring in the first trimester. But even if we allowed those arguments to go unchallenged, what about those 113,000, for which only the grossest ignorance of the facts or the grossest disregard for the lives of other human beings could account? Here in one year are 113,000 exhibits of a worldview that says, "Life is meaningful only when it doesn't interfere with my desires." The incidence of post-abortion distress among women of whatever stage of terminated pregnancy shows that not everyone is capable of living so callously.

Disregard for human life also shows itself in the disrespect being shown for one another's bodies. At a recent seminar conducted at a penitentiary by the international Prison Fellowship ministry for inmates approaching release, a volunteer asked a small group of men about the pressures and temptations they expected to face when they returned to the street. The prisoners mentioned several anticipated problems. "What about sexual desires?" the volunteer prompted.

One man, a Christian active in the Bible studies, nodded. All the rest shook their heads. No, they responded, this was not something they worried about.

"I've got a girlfriend," one explained. "We're not that close, but we help each other out, and she gives me sex when I want it." The man was not trying to be smug or humorous, nor did he express the least bit of embarrassment at this evident lack of feeling toward his sex partner. Probing further, the leader found that the young man truly did not conceive that such a relationship might not be perfectly moral or healthy for either him or his friend. Two other men were equally unblushing in assuming that life was supposed to be promiscuous. "I use a condom," each explained in turn. The volunteer, a veteran of work in jails and prisons for many years, was hardly surprised that the men planned to have sex outside marriage. He did become thoughtful about the lack of meaning they attached to the most intimate relationship between human beings. "What struck me about these men is the sheer ignorance that there could be any other kind of life. They have committed crimes, but each is intelligent, and the one with the girlfriend is serious, articulate, and from a relatively well-off background. They represent a cross-section of our culture."

In that same culture an organization called, ironically, the North American Man/Boy Love Association (NAMBLA), now openly represents the rights of pedophiles in the United States and Canada, proclaiming that we prudes have inhibited natural, healthy sexual activities between men and the young objects of their desires.

Abortions, "mercy killing," using a woman or child to gratify sexual needs, active homosexuality—these are hardly new tendencies. What is new is that in Western Judeo-Christian culture none of these things were considered acceptable behavior until we convinced ourselves that we are qualitatively no different from a community of overachieving amoebas. Slowly society has been conditioned, and is continuing to be conditioned, to tolerate, accept, and even value such "modernity." What once was done in hiding is out of the closet. This great divide occurred largely because of the biggest lie to ever come down the pike, a lie that has done and is doing more harm than any other intellectual theory that I know of. I think most people, including most Christians, are abysmally naïve when it comes to understanding how the theory of evolution contributed to all this misery. Evolution devalues humanity. Underneath its scientific facade, the doctrines of the evolutionary worldview demand that the strong survive, the weak must move aside, and that ultimately none of it matters much. Why should not the ends, whether pleasure or peace, justify all means necessary and convenient?

The eyes of the world were on a hot courtroom in Tennessee back in 1925 when Clarence Darrow called to the stand his opponent in the trial of John Scopes, a trial held to see whether evolution might be acceptable in the schools of the country. The great orator William Jennings Bryan was that opponent, and when Bryan had taken the oath and his seat in the box, Darrow asked Bryan if he realized that in his home state of Nebraska there had lived a whole race of men 1 million years ago. Bryan said he didn't realize anything of the sort, and he didn't believe it, either. So Darrow brought in Dr. Henry Fairfield Osborn of the American Museum of Natural History, the most respected paleontologist in America. Yes, Dr. Osborn verified, just three years prior, in 1922, evidence of a whole race of people had been discovered to have lived in Nebraska a million years ago. Bryan was dumbfounded.

The great con?

The discovery was made by a man named Harold Cooke, who christened the find, in scientific terminology, *Hesperopithecus haroldcookii*. Most called it "Western ape-man." Around the world drawings and recon-structions of "Western ape-man" appeared in museums and schools, showing *Hesperopithecus haroldcookii* in all his glory, sitting around the fire with his family, with a club over his shoulder. Everyone knew exactly what he looked like.

What was the great paleontological discovery that introduced us to our ancient ancestors? It was a tooth—not a skull with teeth, not a jawbone and teeth, nor several teeth. It was one tooth. Sometime later, in the same area, they discovered another, identical tooth, this time connected to a jawbone—the jawbone of an extinct pig or peccary. Creation-science researcher Dr. Duane Gish said, "I believe this is a case in which a scientist made a man out of a pig and a pig made a monkey out of a scientist!" Thanks in part to the Scopes trial, the pig made a monkey out of all of us.

The search for human origins has been a comedy of such errors. In 1959 Dr. W. R. Thompson, an entomologist who for years was director of the Commonwealth Institute of Biological Control in Ottawa, Canada, wrote in the foreword to the centennial edition of Charles Darwin's *Origin of Species*:

> This situation, where men rally to the defense of a doctrine they are unable to define scientifically, much less demonstrate with scientific rigor, attempting to maintain its credit with the public by the suppression of criticism and the elimination of difficulties, is abnormal and undesirable in science. . . . The success of Darwinism was accompanied by a decline in scientific integrity.

A young man who took a course in anthropology at the University of Florida told me he was very surprised that at the end of the course his professor had the integrity to tell the class that all that they had been told during the whole semester was purely speculation. She did not have one single fact to back it up. Dr. T. N. Tahmisian, a physiologist for the Atomic Energy Commission, said: "Scientists who go about teaching that evolution is a fact of life are great con men, and the story they are telling may be the greatest hoax ever."

I often have given my own opinion of evolution and those who teach it as the irrefutable truth. The purpose of this book is to look at God, not to slam scientists, even those who may deserve it. I do not think evolutionists have set out to perpetrate the greatest hoax in human history. I think they are men and women of faith, who fervently hold a worldview and enthusiastically evangelize for it. They honestly believe they are right and I am wrong, and they read and interpret and teach the facts on the basis of their assumption that evolution is the way it must have happened. For some, including such founders of materialist science as Darwin and Ernst Haeckl, it may be argued that their science sprouted from their intense personal animosity toward Christianity. But they did not, I assume, deliberately set out to mislead. Their rebellious hearts, their prejudice, and their worldview assumptions blinded them, just as Paul said in Romans 1:18–23.

Aldous Huxley, leading atheist and evolutionist and author of *Brave New World*, said this:

> I had motives for not wanting the world to have meaning; consequently assumed that it had none, and was able without any difficulty to find satisfying reasons for this assumption. . . . For myself, as, no doubt, for most of my contemporaries, the philosophy of mean-

inglessness was essentially an instrument of liberation. The liberation we desired was simultaneously liberation from a certain political and economic system [capitalism] and liberation from a certain system of morality. We objected to the morality because it interfered with our sexual freedom.

Another of the famous Huxleys, Julian, has been equally forthright about the reasons for the immediate acceptance of Darwin's book, *Origin of Species*: "We all jumped at the *Origin* because the idea of God interfered with our sexual mores."

The great revolution?

At this writing the final outcome of the breakup of the Soviet Bloc remains years away. Some new totalitarianism may emerge with promises of economic and social stability to the nations born at the beginning of the 1990s. Nearly three-quarters of a century of economic, social, cultural, and religious repression will not be washed away quickly. Neither will the revolution in worldview unleashed by the events of the last decade be undone. In those early days of openness American Christian booksellers were invited for the first time to show their wares at the Moscow Book Fair. One company brought 50,000 Russian language Bibles to give away. The police stopped them from giving away their Bibles for several hours at the show because such a mob of people rushed the booth that every aisle of the Book Fair turned to gridlock. The police told them to give Bibles away for one hour, stop for two hours, and resume for another hour. The officials were not trying to prevent the distribution. They simply wished to keep the aisles open and to prevent injury. Nearby, Madalyn Murray O'Hair was displaying her wares at the

American Atheist Society booth. Someone who was there told me that virtually no one stopped to even see what she had to offer. They knew all too well.

Those of us who have followed life in these countries have heard countless stories of the spiritual revolution that accompanied the political and economic changes. One of the sad elements of this miracle has been that great numbers of Western cultists and radical preachers have flooded into the countries to peddle their own agenda, so many that the government was forced to consider reestablishing restrictions. Even American speakers with something substantive to say alienated listeners by offering great, inspiring messages full of advice without love or understanding of the real spiritual issues the people wanted to hear about.

But there were others, such as one young Michigan layman, who did make a difference. David Marvin was invited, much to his surprise, on a trip to Romania in early 1993. David hurriedly did his best to put together a series of messages, praying that the Lord would show him why he had been given this opportunity. Two things utterly changed his life as soon as he set foot on Romanian soil, causing him to discard those feverishly studied sermons. First, he encountered unimaginable deprivation and poverty. But second, and more important, in the midst of near starvation Christians were the most generous, disciplined, spiritually alive, and joyful he had ever known. In the comparatively well-off home in which he stayed there was not enough money to buy fuel, and the temperature hovered only slightly above freezing. But any extra money after the most basic needs were provided was dropped into a jar on the table so that it would be available to give to those more needy. The $1500 he took with him to distribute was given to a church that had nothing, and the church immediately gave most of the gift to a visiting

Russian pastor whose people were worse off—this in a country where hatred for Russians runs deep and pre-dates the Soviet occupation. It didn't take long to learn the reason for this revolutionary Christian disciple-ship. The Romanian church had been nurtured under the persecution of an atheistic worldview. In such a desert the smallest stream of spiritual water offered soul-quenching nourishment. God was not just there. The Creator of all was seen at work daily among his people.

David tells of his experience: "I learned that I was not sent to Romania to minister to those people. They ministered to me by teaching me what was missing from my own spiritual life and the lives of most American Christians. I could not stand before them to speak without breaking down in tears of shame for the way we have allowed our material gifts to pull our eyes off the Giver."

By the end of his month in Romania, people were crowding to hear the man they called "Dahveed Ahmereeka—the man who cries." We too need to hear what David Marvin said in those meetings: "Some day soon you people of Romania will have a better life, with more money to spend. That will be when you will face your greatest danger. Never become like the people of the West. Reject our lifestyle. Don't lose your hard-won consciousness of God. You are so rich; we are so poor." David now takes that message of shame to his own impoverished countrymen.

It was in a barren wilderness that Moses looked ahead and saw the danger of neglecting the Creator of heaven and earth:

And it shall be, when the LORD thy God shall have brought thee into the land which he sware unto thy fathers, to Abraham, to Isaac, and to Jacob, to give thee great and goodly cities, which thou buildest not, And houses full of all good things, which thou filledst not, and wells digged, which thou diggedst not, vineyards and olive trees, which thou plantedst not; when thou shalt have eaten and be full; Then beware lest thou forget the LORD, which brought thee forth out of the land of Egypt, from the house of bondage. [Deuteronomy 6:10–12]

Looking back on those years, the writer of Psalm 106:13–15 tells the result of forgetfulness toward God: "They soon forgat his works; they waited not for his counsel: But lusted exceedingly in the wilderness, and tempted God in the desert. And he gave them their request; but sent leanness into their soul."

The wasting disease

How we need a Romanian revolution in worldview! The citizens of the former Soviet states, even those citizens who have not turned to Christ, have experienced the shattering of a society built on the worldview that we are not creatures living in a magnificently created world that was made by an infinitely creative God.

In the late 1950s Dr. Ernest Gordon, dean emeritus of Princeton University Chapel, was invited to address the senior class of an English department in a city high school. He arrived at the office of the assistant headmaster, who guided him to the lecture hall. Twenty years later he was invited to speak at the same school, only it was not the same school at all. The assistant headmaster's office had become the security command post. Corridors and classrooms were monitored by police officers. Dr. Gordon wrote:

I interpret this scene as evidence of the endtimes of a civilization that had once benefited from the Christian worldview, one that exalted creation and people, and provided the ideals essential for an authentic education. I recognize that civilization does not create Christians. However, the community of faith created and still creates the civility that is evidence of civilization. That demoralized school is the tragic consequence of a society's rejection of the biblical worldview that provided the intellectual dynamic of Western education. What is education but an expression of the prevailing culture?

A newspaper article quoted Harvard scientist Stephen Jay Gould, a leading evolutionist, with this equally disturbing statement: "We're an afterthought, a little accidental twig." I don't know what you do with little accidental twigs that fall on your lawn. I pile them in a heap and throw them in the garbage. That is, I guess, Gould's view of life. We are nothing more than little accidental twigs. The writer of the newspaper article made the aside that "there is nothing quite like a conversation with Stephen Jay Gould to knock a little evolutionary humility into a person." That is more than a little humility. When set alongside the other evidence it seems more the symptom of a wasting disease that is destroying the significance of humanity. The evolutionary worldview immersing our society has declared all-out war with *teleology*—the idea that things exist for a purpose. We already have talked about the Christian's view of the teleology for each human being: to glorify and enjoy God forever. The writers of the *Westminster Confession* described a similar teleology for the creation of all other things, particularly humanity:

It pleased God the Father, Son, and Holy Ghost, for the manifestation of the glory of his eternal power, wisdom, and goodness, in the beginning to create or make of nothing the world, and all things therein, whether visible or invisible, in the space of six days, and all very good. After God had made all other creatures, he created man, male and female, with reasonable and immortal souls, endued with knowledge, righteousness, and true holiness, after his own image.

God is triune, infinite, eternal, and unchangeable in his wisdom, power, holiness, justice, goodness, and truth. See how all of that fits into the Christian's world-and-life view.

Have ye not known? have ye not heard? hath it not been told you from the beginning? have ye not understood from the foundations of the earth? It is he that sitteth upon the circle of the earth, and the inhabitants thereof are as grasshoppers; that stretcheth out the heavens as a curtain, and spreadeth them out as a tent to dwell in. . . . Lift up your eyes on high, and behold who hath created these things, that bringeth out their host by number: he calleth them all by names by the greatness of his might, for that he is strong in power; not one faileth. . . . Hast thou not known? hast thou not heard, that the everlasting God, the LORD, the Creator of the ends of the earth, fainteth not, neither is weary? there is no searching of his understanding. [Isaiah 40:21–22, 26, 28]

The theologians at Westminster and Isaiah agree that the creation and direct revelation of the Bible teach us three magnificent things about the Creator God. First, he is powerful; second, we cannot fathom his wisdom and understanding; and third, he is good. God's is not a strength that must be renewed with rest. His wisdom forgets not where a star has wandered off to. This is not an excellence that begins the job and leaves it half-finished. He still is involved, unwearied and everlasting. What else do we know about God that applies to our culture? Here are just a few things:

This is a Creator who should knock more humility into us than Stephen Jay Gould's ridiculous assessment:

> The LORD said unto him, Who hath made man's mouth? or who maketh the dumb, or deaf, or the seeing, or the blind? have not I the LORD? [Exodus 4:11]

> You give life to everything, and the multitudes of heaven worship you. [Nehemiah 9:6b NIV]

> Thou hast possessed my reins: thou hast covered me in my mother's womb. I will praise thee; for I am fearfully and wonderfully made: marvellous are thy works; and that my soul knoweth right well. [Psalm 139:13–14]

> The rich and poor meet together: the LORD is the maker of them all. [Proverbs 22:2]

> The heaven is my throne, and the earth is my footstool: . . . but to this man will I look, even to him that is poor and of a contrite spirit, and trembleth at my word. [Isaiah 66:1–2]

This is a Creator whose works are good:

> God saw every thing that he had made, and, behold, it was very good. [Genesis 1:31a]

> How manifold are thy works! in wisdom hast thou made them all: the earth is full of thy riches. Thou openest thine hand, they are filled with good. [Psalm 104:24, 28b]

For every creature of God is good, and nothing to be refused, if it be received with thanksgiving. [1 Timothy 4:4]

This is a Creator worthy of all my worship and praise:

For great is the LORD, and greatly to be praised: he also is to be feared above all gods. [1 Chronicles 16:25]

Let them praise the name of the LORD, for he commanded, and they were created. He hath also stablished them for ever and ever: he hath made a decree which shall not pass. [Psalm 148:5–6]

But to us there is but one God, the Father, of whom are all things, and we in him; and one Lord Jesus Christ, by whom are all things, and we by him. [1 Corinthians 8:6]

This is a Creator who re-creates in Jesus Christ:

In that day will I make a covenant for them with the beasts of the field, and with the fowls of heaven, and with the creeping things of the ground: and I will break the bow and the sword and the battle out of the earth, and will make them to lie down safely. And I will betroth thee unto me for ever; yea, I will betroth thee unto me in righteousness, and in judgment, and in lovingkindness, and in mercies. [Hosea 2:18–19]

For I reckon that the sufferings of this present time are not worthy to be compared with the glory which shall be revealed in us. For the earnest expectation of the creature waiteth for the manifestation of the sons of God. For the creature was made subject to vanity, not willingly, but by reason of him who hath subjected the same in hope, Because the creature itself also shall be delivered from the bondage of corruption into the glorious liberty of the children of God. [Romans 8:18–21]

God . . . hath in these last days spoken unto us by his Son, whom he hath appointed heir of all things, by whom also he made the worlds; Who being the brightness of his glory, and the express image of his person, and upholding all things by the word of his power, when he had by himself purged our sins, sat down on the right hand of the Majesty on high. [Hebrews 1:1–3]

He that sat upon the throne said, Behold, I make all things new. [Revelation 21:5a]

The re-creation revolution

The revolution that counts grows not from the teaching that a person has evolved. It grows from the re-creation that *revolves* a person's life a 180-degree direction change from that in which he or she has been going. Quite frankly, I fear for the future of the West, a culture whose engine is fueled by the big lie. On the other hand, I am supremely confident in the re-creating power of God the Creator. How ironic, but also how like God, that we must now find our Christian discipleship model in the lives of former Eastern Bloc Christians like those David Marvin met in Romania, those who have lived so long under the thumb of atheism. In the ashes of the most disastrous worldview in history his re-creating power has been fashioning something of quietly spectacular loveliness.

But now we need a similar re-creation revolution in our midst, one that takes us off the sidelines and empowers us with a message of shame that we have been pulled away from God by the evolution revolution. When God first breathed life into humankind he gave us what is called the "cultural mandate." In Genesis 1:28b we have a commission given to us as creatures created in his image in knowledge, righteousness, and true holiness. Our mandate is:

> Be fruitful, and multiply, and replenish the earth, and subdue it: and have dominion over the fish of the sea, and over the fowl of the air, and over every living thing that moveth upon the earth.

Fruitfulness to Adam and Eve meant to have children. Fruitfulness to a church in the late twentieth century means we need to reproduce and multiply spiritually. You who are unbelievers are called by the Creator of heaven and earth to revolve, turning from a worldview of meaninglessness and the big lie, to a worldview of purpose and truth. We are called to do nothing less than to glorify God and to enjoy him forever. We who are already children of God in Christ Jesus are called to go and make disciples. And we also are called to involvement in the declaration of God's glory in the arts, in education, in culture, in business—in every sphere of life.

The Bible's principles apply to the individual, the church, the family, and the school, but too often we have stopped there. God also has principles that apply to the artist, to the writer, to the factory worker, to the senator, to the physician, to the lawyer, to every human being on the planet. The cultural mandate points us at the world in all that we are and says, "Be fruitful. Subdue. Bring every cranny of life under the Word of God as far as you are enabled to do so. Offer all to the glory of God."

Is anyone in control out there?

God, the great Creator of all things, doth uphold, direct, dispose, and govern all creatures, actions, and things, from the greatest even to the least, by his most wise and holy providence, according to his infallible foreknowledge and the free and immutable counsel of his own will, to the praise of the glory of his wisdom, power, justice, goodness, and mercy. [Westminster Confession of Faith, chapter 5]

7

Plan, Power, and Providence

t is, without doubt, the most popular religious program ever to hit TV. Millions of television sets tune in each week to watch a glamorous high priestess, who always looks somewhat like Vanna White, gracefully push the necessary buttons on a glass altar filled with swirling white objects. All of the people have offered their sacrifices at the local gas station and grocery store. On whom will the gods of fate bestow beneficence? Seven balls—possibly white to symbolize the ethical purity of the religion's rulers, the state lottery commission—dance through a pneumatic tube and display the numbers that will mean a life of total ease and fabulous wealth for some lucky worshiper.

The next day a report appears in the daily newspaper. Some needy soul has been plucked from obscure poverty and is on her way, even as the reporter interviews her, to buy a Maserati. The fate gods have smiled. The fate gods are good. Bow now before the fate gods and buy thirty tickets for this week's $22 million jackpot.

Is playing the lottery worship? Rather, is it idolatry? Yes, I believe it is, and more than a little foolish. I would not like to lay money against such odds. Governments callously play on popular greed. Impoverished people who have trouble putting food on their table voluntarily pay precious dollars with little realistic hope of return. The lottery madness lends a whole new dimension to Jesus' words: "For where your treasure is, there will your heart be also" (Matthew 6:21).

There is no Super Lotto god, and I should let everyone in on a secret about these games of "chance": *They are rigged—every one of them.* Winners were chosen untold ages back within the intricate warp and woof of the sovereign plan of God. If the sovereign God who is recognized in the Bible exists, then chance or fate does not exist. The two are mutually exclusive. In *Fiddler on the Roof,* bemused Tevye asks God: "Would it upset some eternal plan if I were a wealthy man?" God's eter-

> *Remember this, fix it in mind, take it to heart, you rebels. Remember the former things, those of long ago; I am God, and there is no other; I am God, and there is none like me. I make known the end from the beginning, from ancient times, what is still to come. I say: My purpose will stand, and I will do all that I please.* [Isaiah 46: 8–10 NIV]

nal plan for the universe is infinitely larger than whether
Tevye becomes financially comfortable, but Tevye's
wealth might have ramifications to that plan that he cannot foresee. It just could upset some eternal plan if he
were a wealthy man. Tevye lacks the wisdom to know.

Sovereignty means God's providential rule over all
lives stands within the scope of a divine plan. His
divine authority will carry it through. "I trusted in thee,
O LORD: I said, Thou art my God. My times are in thy
hand" (Psalm 31:14–15a). Scripture teaches that my
times are in his hands, and it would be odd if there were
any other possibility. The God who weaves amino acids
of the genetic code inside the structure of each living
cell might be expected to govern how the aggregates
of those cells while away their hours.

Fatalism?

The sovereignty of God has never been and never will
be a popular subject. Some charge that this doctrine
strikes a fatalist's pose: If God commands minutiae, we
are simply puppets, dancing out a rehearsed scenario.
Others will add that such a view destroys all pretense
of human free will. Still others allege that if God exerts
such control he must be a monstrous tyrant, allowing
the terrors of life to unfold without intervention. Could
God be deaf to the cries of people in pain?

Since the beginning of creation, the creature has
sought to usurp the place of the Creator. Lucifer, the
angel of light, first sought to grasp the divine prerogatives. He and a great multitude of angels with him
had to be evicted from heaven. Grasping for God's prerogatives also occasioned the human banishment from
Eden; two pretenders to the throne insisted that their
own plan was obviously more pleasant and practical

than that fixed by their Lord. Yet the plan of God drew one line before them, saying: "Thus far you will go, and no farther. . . . If you eat of that fruit you will die" (see Genesis 2:17).

The skeptic H. G. Wells said that the world is like a great play, produced and directed by God. As the curtain goes up, all is lovely to behold. The characters are fantastically beautiful—a delight to eye and ear. All goes well until the leading man steps on the hem of the leading lady's dress. She trips and falls into a chair, knocking over a lamp that pushes a table into the side wall. This knocks over the back scenery, which brings the entire set crashing down in chaos on the heads of the actors. Meanwhile, God frantically runs to and fro, pulling strings and shouting orders, trying desperately to restore order to the chaos. He is unable to do so. Poor God.

Modern religion prefers such a limited God because this God is not blamable for evil and suffering. "Either God is not good or he is not powerful," runs the popular sentiment. Since most people are unwilling to believe God is not good, they conclude that he is doing the best that he can. He tries and fails. Which horn of the dilemma do you choose?

May I suggest that the God of Scripture hardly fits either description. He is omnipotent and has all power. Therefore his plan will be worked out. He is holy, and therefore his plan is morally right. He is infinite, eternal, and unchangeable in wisdom, power, holiness, justice, goodness, and truth. Therefore his is not the *merely* omnipotent force of fatalism. The biblical picture denies fatalism, because fatalism puts all that happens in the hands of an impersonal force, while Scripture places it in the hands of a Father who is all righteous, wise, and merciful. Fatalism rules out second causes. The stars, fates, gods, or whatever, pull the strings of fate directly. The Bible establishes second causes, declaring that every human being freely does whatever he or she *pleases* at any given moment of time. Unfortunately what pleases the individual outside of Christ is limited to direct disobedience against God. The natural state since the fall has been worthlessness—slavery to sin. "What iniquity have your fathers found in me, that they are gone far from me?" asked Jeremiah. In their freedom these people "have walked after vanity [or worthless idols], and are become vain [worthless]" (Jeremiah 2:5). Romans 1:24 adds that "God also *gave them up* to uncleanness through the lusts of their own hearts." That does not signal the creature's veto power over the plans of the Almighty, but rather a frantic chasing around in circles that accomplishes nothing.

Captain of a ship of fools

How ludicrous and blasphemous to think that the God who by the authority of his word governs creation steps meekly aside as his rebellious creature screams: "I am the master of my fate and the captain of my soul." There is a word for the attempt to master my fate. That word is *futility*. "Has not the LORD Almighty determined that the people's labor is only fuel for the fire, that the nations exhaust themselves for nothing?" asked the prophet Habakkuk (2:13 NIV).

During a flood a reporter was sent out in a boat to find out how the stranded people were faring. Floating down what only days before had been a street, he noticed a woman who was perched on the edge of her roof, staring out into the swirling waters. She said nothing as he climbed up to join her but noticed that she was watching a hat drift with the current.

Or was it? Suddenly the hat turned and started back upstream. The reporter stared in amazement as the hat bobbed back and forth by the house, first with the flow of the water and then against it.

"I just don't understand that at all," he remarked.

"Oh, that's my husband," the woman responded. "He said he was going to mow the lawn come hell or high water."

As futile as mowing grass in a flood is the scramble for life that does not take God into account. "Except the LORD build the house, they labour in vain that build it: except the LORD keep the city, the watchman waketh but in vain" (Psalm 127:1). Most of the world's most graciously appointed mansions hide lives colored by sorrow and meaninglessness. What really is the point of laboring for wealth that requires intricate security systems to protect and may vanish with the next downturn of the stock market? Why go to all the trouble accumulating at all, if there is nothing more lasting than today's work and next weekend's party?

Those wealthy people who have paid large fortunes to have their cadavers cryogenically frozen hope someday to be resurrected to eternal life through the next miracle of technology. Yet immortal existence would become hell itself if life offered no more than sustained breath. It is interesting how many horror novelists write plots fantasizing what it would be like to be cursed with the inability to die. We innately realize that this is a horror, because we were made to glorify and enjoy God—to participate in a sovereign plan that gives eternal worth. The story of the human fall into sin ends on just this sad note. The human residents of Eden are driven into exile into a world of thorns and futile labor. An angel with a flaming sword stands watch over the forbidden entrance to the home from which the man and woman have been evicted (Genesis

3:22–24). But it is not for punishment that this angelic guard watches, but as a mercy. For God declares that the human being must never be allowed to reach for the fruit of the tree of life while in this state of sin. That fruit was made to give eternal life, not ongoing existence entrapped in the futility of sinful flesh.

God's providence is not only logical and true; it is the only view that gives life worth. Psalm 127, which speaks of the futility of building houses and watching cities without God's partnership, contrasts that vain scramble with the blessedness of resting in God's infinitely meaningful purpose: "It is vain for you to rise up early, to sit up late, to eat the bread of sorrows: for so he giveth his beloved sleep" (v. 2).

Explaining providence

Christian confessions affirm that God's good plan rules his universe through his acts of creation and providence. Creation we have talked about in previous chapters. But just as not all agree on what creation means, there is considerable difference of opinion regarding providence. Its double-minded tentativeness contributes to the church's lack of confidence in an uncertain world. Nothing should give us so hearty a hope on the front lines of a culture war with sensualism, humanism, and materialism as a solid understanding of God's sovereignty over all.

Providence refers to God's omniscient foreknowledge of what will happen; it also depicts God's omnipotent governance of history. One of the most beautiful and pastoral descriptions of God's providence was written into the *Belgic Confession of Faith* by Guido deBres, who later gave his life at the stake, a martyr for the Reformation of the Netherlands. For deBres the key to God's providence lies in his constancy. He will not walk off and forget his creation, nor his rebellious creatures:

> We believe that the same good God, after He had created all things, did not forsake them or give them up to fortune or chance, but that He rules and governs them according to His holy will, so that nothing happens in this world without His appointment; nevertheless, God neither is the Author of nor can be charged with the sins which are committed. For His power and goodness are so great and incomprehensible that He orders and executes His work in the most excellent and just manner, even then when devils and wicked men act unjustly. And as to what He does surpassing human understanding, we will not curiously inquire into farther than our capacity will admit of; but with the greatest humility and reverence adore the righteous judgments of God, which are hid from us, contenting ourselves that we are pupils of Christ, to learn only those things which He has revealed to us in His word, without transgressing these limits.

Another document of faith, the *Heidelberg Catechism*, stands alongside the *Belgic Confession*. For the question, "What dost thou mean by the providence of God?" the *Catechism* answers:

> The almighty and every where present power of God; whereby, as it were by His hand, He upholds and governs heaven, earth, and all creatures so that herbs and grass, rain and drought, fruitful and barren years, meat and drink, health and sickness, riches and poverty, yea, all things come, not by chance, but by His fatherly hand.

The *Westminster Confession*'s statement on divine providence heads this chapter. The *Shorter Catechism* answers "What are God's works of providence?":

> God's works of providence are, his most holy, wise, and
> powerful preserving and governing all his creatures
> and all their actions.

In these human explanations lies the exquisite biblical answer to those who would see God sickly or
wicked or an impersonal force. Each says that God:

1. *preserves creation.* The sun will not suddenly
   flame out and send the earth hurtling into a black
   hole while God has his back turned.
2. *governs all of creation and the natural phenomena.* The stars in our own neighborhood, and
   those of every other galaxy equally come under
   God's command, as does the sparrow that falls to
   the ground (Matthew 10:29).
3. *governs human thoughts and actions.* God so
   rules in history so that nothing occurs that is not
   taken into account in God's plan. In fact he foresees and arranges the flow of second causes in history and each individual life according to his infinitely wise will. Yet the evil that occurs among
   those second causes arises only from the bondage
   of sin and death upon creation. God uses them for
   his purposes, but he is not their author.

The logic of a God in control

The preserving governance of God is agreed to by any
theist who believes in a Creator as opposed to a
mindless, evolutionary, pantheistic force. Belief in the
preservation of creation certainly is not much of a
stretch for someone who believes in a Being capable of

creating the universe in the first place. Could not the designer and manufacturer of a product manage to write and follow the maintenance manual? There are many who disbelieve in a God who is this powerful over creation, but their problem involves disbelieving the more basic assumptions that there exists a Designer and Manufacturer.

Most people with any faith in, and understanding of, the God of the Bible willingly take the second step as well. If God created and maintains, it follows that he established and administers the laws that govern the natural order of that creation.

I should suspect that God, if he desired, could suspend those laws. If it pleased him he could stop or even reverse the motion of the earth relative to the sun (Joshua 10:12–14; Isaiah 38:7–8). And if he could do that he certainly could, without working up a sweat, manipulate the weather to deny rain or send down hail in judgment (Exodus 9:22–26; Joshua 10:11; 1 Kings 17:1; 18:41–45; 2 Chronicles 6:26–27; Revelation 8:7–9). He could manipulate or even create new natural phenomena to turn the day dark (Exodus 10:21–23; Luke 23:44–45) or to cause the light from a distant star to appear on the earth at just the moment and in just the right quadrant of the sky to guide travelers where he wished them to go (Matthew 2:1–2, 9). And if he could do that, I seriously doubt it would be an unreasonable burden for him to calm a storm, walk on water, or control the healing process of the body (for example, Matthew 14:22–27; 15:30–31; Mark 4:35–41). Those who are troubled by such possibilities have a problem somewhat deeper in their concept of God than simply disbelief in what are called "miracles."

It is the governing of thoughts and actions that divides. We should be able to agree that if a God can do such things as already described, he can act with

understanding and influence over the affairs of humanity. Certainly he can, for example, exert control over
the environmental and genetic and social influences in
a life. Surely an omniscient God foresees the individual's future reactions to various situations, particularly
if he enjoys total perception of the individual's personality and thought processes. And he would be able
to influence, help, guide, or overrule the individual's
actions by controlling the flow of experiences and influences that swirl around a life and cause the person to
constantly make choices. Certainly in the Christian the
indwelling power of the Holy Spirit undeniably influences actions. In such a scenario we might even say
that sovereign governance does not truly interfere with
the person's "freedom" to choose, so long as the individual is quite free to pick from among available
options at each point along the way.

Some Christian traditions zealously guard our freedom as human beings to make choices based on our
will. They are afraid that a God who exercises sovereign authority must be a puppet master who sends people to heaven or hell on a whim and is chargeable with
all evil that occurs in the world. Others are zealous to
protect God's omnipotent control over all people and
his mercy in enabling the lost to turn to him in repentance. Our sources for resolving such issues are limited. As deBres wisely wrote,

> And as to what He does surpassing human under-
> standing, we will not curiously inquire into farther than
> our capacity will admit of; but with the greatest humil-
> ity and reverence adore the righteous judgments of
> God, which are hid from us, contenting ourselves that
> we are pupils of Christ, to learn only those things which
> He has revealed to us in His word, without transgress-
> ing these limits.

We can, however, know *some* things, for the Bible teaches us much about who God is, who we are, and how he acts. We must uphold all that the Bible teaches us. First, free or not, people do make choices freely, based on their will. Yet it is equally clear that God does rule and overrule in the affairs of humanity.

The power and the plan

The Bible does not equivocate about the providential design and authority of the Almighty to control everything from the galaxy to the atom. He governs the angels in heaven, the inhabitants of earth, and the kings and fortunes of nations. He raises them up and casts them down. He brings one to power and removes that power by the stroke of his hand, working through second causes.

The right of lordship

God has the prerogatives to micromanage history, not simply because he has the biggest, most omnipotent club to hold over the heads of people, but because we his creatures belong to him by right. "It is he that hath made us, and not we ourselves; we are his people, and the sheep of his pasture" (Psalm 100:3). "O LORD, I know that the way of man is not in himself: it is not in man that walketh to direct his steps" (Jeremiah 10:23).

There is a current teaching in many churches that declares that one can enjoy the fruits of salvation in the atoning sacrifice of Jesus Christ on the cross without accepting Jesus as personal Lord. That is bunk on three counts. First, Jesus is Lord by right of creatorship and demands submission to his authority whether one accepts or rejects him as Savior. God calls sinful people to acknowledge his lordship but makes it clear the lordship extends to every person—repentant sinner or rebel:

> Look unto me, and be ye saved, all the ends of the earth: for I am God, and there is none else. I have sworn by myself, the word is gone out of my mouth in righteousness, and shall not return, That unto me every knee shall bow, every tongue shall swear. Surely, shall one say, in the LORD I have righteousness and strength: even to him shall men come; and all that are incensed against him shall be ashamed. [Isaiah 45:22–24]

Second, Jesus is Lord by right of his conquest over Satan, the fulfillment of God's sovereign plan. Philippians 2:9–11 (and Romans 14:9–12) says that because Jesus put off his glory as God and humbled himself to death on the cross,

> Wherefore God also hath highly exalted him, and given him a name which is above every name: That at the name of Jesus every knee should bow, of things in heaven, and things in earth, and things under the earth; And that every tongue should confess that Jesus Christ is Lord, to the glory of God the Father.

Third, Jesus possesses lordship most particularly and definitively over the lives of those who have become his personal people through the gift of salvation. The apostle Paul makes this especially plain, as in 1 Corinthians 6:20: "Ye are bought with a price." Paul tells all Christians in Romans 6:20, 22, "When ye were the servants of sin, ye were free from righteousness. But now being made free from sin, and become servants to God, ye have your fruit unto holiness, and the end everlasting life." In Ephesians 2:10 Paul describes the way God has re-created us and redesigned our lives around Jesus Christ so that his lordship might make us a blessing to others: "For we are his workmanship, created in Christ Jesus unto good works, which God hath before ordained that we should walk in them." If we are truly in Christ, Paul adds, his power as Lord works within us (Ephesians 3:20).

Those are the benefits of accepting a plan that includes the lordship of Christ. For those who want the Savior without the Lord, rejecting one means rejecting the other: "Wherefore we receiving a kingdom which cannot be moved, let us have grace, whereby we may serve God acceptably with reverence and godly fear: For our God is a consuming fire" (Hebrews 12:28–29).

The freedom of lordship

God has the prerogatives of authority over every action and thought because that is how he established the universe to function. The difference between us and God is that we are made for his ownership while he has perfect freedom to act in concert with his will. Isaiah 46:10 relates God's ultimate claim that "I will do as I please." He alone makes that statement without fear of contradiction. And the Bible extends that statement over our individual lives and actions.

> The LORD killeth, and maketh alive: he bringeth down to the grave, and bringeth up. The LORD maketh poor, and maketh rich: he bringeth low, and lifteth up. He raiseth up the poor out of the dust, and lifteth up the beggar from the dunghill, to set them among princes, and to make them inherit the throne of glory: for the

pillars of the earth are the LORD's, and he hath set the world upon them. [1 Samuel 2:6–8]

He shall break in pieces mighty men without number, and set others in their stead. [Job 34:24]

No one from the east or the west or from the desert can exalt a man. But it is God who judges: He brings one down, he exalts another. [Psalm 75:6–7 NIV]

He raiseth up the poor out of the dust, and lifteth the needy out of the dunghill; That he may set him with princes, even with the princes of his people. He maketh the barren woman to keep house, and to be a joyful mother of children. Praise ye the LORD. [Psalm 113:7–9]

A man's heart deviseth his way: but the LORD directeth his steps. [Proverbs 16:9]

There are many devices in a man's heart; nevertheless the counsel of the LORD, that shall stand. [Proverbs 19:21]

This is the purpose that is purposed upon the whole earth: and this is the hand that is stretched out upon all the nations. For the LORD of hosts hath purposed, and who shall disannul it? and his hand is stretched out, and who shall turn it back? [Isaiah 14:26–27]

Freedom under providence

A lack of human freedom may bother others, but I am quite thankful for it, for I am not altogether competent to manage my own affairs. First, God's perfect freedom means I can come to him with my petitions, knowing that he is more than capable of giving whatever I ask, however immense that request may seem to me. Second, in his perfect understanding and care of my life, God knows whether what I ask for is wise or frivolous and even detrimental. So he also is able to say, "No, I have a better plan than you have conceived. I love you too much to give you what you want. But I will provide exactly what you need." Third, sometimes God listens to my petitioning heart and says, "That is something I will give you, but the time is not quite right. Just wait, child; grow up a little more and learn to trust me." And sometimes God listens and says, "Yes. That is something I gladly give. Receive my blessing and follow me on."

Of course this freedom from my own folly means submitting to God's authority when that is precisely the last thing I want. Suppose a doctor breaks the news that I or someone I cherish is facing a painful, debilitating, terminal illness. There is no human hope through medical technology. Now what do I do with God's possible answers to my cry for help? That is when God's freedom will become precious. I can go to him, knowing that he is able to deal with the medical condition immediately and utterly. I can go to him, knowing as well that if he says no to my request for healing it will not be because he is weak or because I lack some magic prayer word formula to make him obey me. It will be because he has a greater plan that I do not see. He has already given me part of the answer to my grief in Romans 8. Paul says that suffering and death continue because of the curse of sin, yet these things can never be out of the Father's control, and they can never separate the sufferer from him. These things will work for good. But if, in my anguish and confusion, I forget or feel unable to accept those realities, and if I become angry with him, God's perfect ability and wisdom will understand what I feel and love and comfort me anyway. And beyond all that I will know that he can give me the grace to bear whatever must be borne.

God's freedom also becomes his great gift when we look at the evil that exists within the world. The Christian is called, as a purchased servant, to stand in the midst of the battle. The purchased servant does not have the options to submit to a world system or to cynically or resignedly stand aside because "That is just the way things are." As God is sovereign, with a plan and power, fatalism can never be the appropriate response. We are empowered by infinite power to do what he has given us to do where he has given us to do it, within the boundaries set by his wisdom, will, and Word. And if we have followed his lead and fall flat on our faces by every human measure of success, we still will have victory in the divine providential perception of things. The battle isn't ours to win but ours to stand.

And if evil vanquishes all apparent hope we should never forget that the providence of God rules beyond our understanding, though Satan throws the forces of hell into the arena. One wicked Egyptian pharaoh thought he was standing firm against the Hebrew God, yet that God said to him: "For this cause have I raised thee up, for to shew in thee my power; and that my name may be declared throughout all the earth. As yet exaltest thou thyself against my people, that thou wilt not let them go?" (Exodus 9:16–17). Proverbs 21:1 tells us that ultimately "the king's heart is in the hand of the LORD, as the rivers of water: he turneth it whithersoever he will."

The power and plan of providence have already won the battle. The kingdom of Jesus is established forever:

> The kings of the earth set themselves, and the rulers take counsel together, against the LORD, and against

his anointed, saying, Let us break their bands asunder, and cast away their cords from us.

He that sitteth in the heavens shall laugh: the LORD shall have them in derision. Then shall he speak unto them in his wrath, and vex them in his sore displeasure. Yet have I set my king upon my holy hill of Zion. [Psalm 2:2–6]

If there is a good God, why . . . ?

Q. What was the providence of God toward man in the estate in which he was created?

A. The providence toward man in the estate in which he was created was the placing him in paradise, appointing him to dress it, giving him liberty to eat of the fruit of the earth; putting the creatures under his dominion, and ordaining marriage for his help; affording him communion with himself; instituting the Sabbath; entering into a covenant of life with him, upon condition of personal, perfect and perpetual obedience, of which the tree of life was a pledge; and forbidding them to eat of the tree of the knowledge of good and evil, upon the pain of death. [Westminster Larger Catechism, question 20]

The Sorcerer's Apprentice

God made man good, and good he remained. We have no sin. Man is incapable of sin. Man cannot depart from holiness.

If Mary Baker Eddy were alive today I doubt she would have written those words. Such a sentiment was popular over 100 years ago in the glow of optimism that humanity was evolving quite nicely. No wonder Mrs. Eddy's Christian Science movement has been on the wane in recent decades, and the old classic liberal Christianity, while still with us in a variety of forms, doesn't make the same old noises as in the late 1800s that "Every day, in every way, I'm getting better and better."

That was before the artillery sounded, and twenty-five allied nations marched off to fight the Central Powers of the Austria-Hungary Empire, the Ottoman Empire, and Bulgaria. Many millions tramped off to the great "war to end all wars," but 10 million never returned; 20 million were wounded at Flanders field, Amiens, and Belleau Wood. When Johnny came marching home, little did he realize that this was only the warm-up for a greater spectacle. This time the arenas were named Dunkirk, Iwo Jima, Normandy, and

Hiroshima. Finally the world was "safe for democracy." But we all know that the world has not been safe for anyone. As these words go onto paper, and probably as you read them, children cry from blown-off limbs, civilians crouch in shelters, and young soldiers face one another in any of several "hot spots." This hardly seems the golden age that our liberal great-grandfathers promised, nor the "age of Aquarius" the 1960s radicals saw in the stars.

Those who do not believe in God have mostly turned from optimism to cynicism to nihilism over the last century. The most optimistic form of irreligion with any real influence on the Western scene is an irrational blend of secular humanism and Eastern mysticism that mostly ignores the issue of evil. But cynics of every stripe sneer at Christians with the taunt: "Where is your God in all of this?"

> *God blessed them, and God said unto them, Be fruitful, and multiply, and replenish the earth, and subdue it: and have dominion over the fish of the sea, and over the fowl of the air, and over every living thing that moveth upon the earth. . . . And God saw every living thing that he had made, and, behold, it was very good.* [Genesis 1:28, 31a]

The invisible gardener

At the beginning of this book we set out on a pilgrimage up into the mountains of life for a closer view of God. It has been all too brief a journey, filled with tantalizing glimpses of glory. Human language offers only childish babbling sounds to communicate the Father, Son, and Holy Spirit, one God—"For of him, and through him, and to him, are all things: to whom be glory for ever. Amen" (Romans 11:36).

Now that we stand on a higher plane, however, we have won a new vantage point from which to observe the world. If you can mentally push through the smog, what do you view? Much is beautiful, isn't it? In book one of his meditational studies of Scripture, *Before the Face of God*, R. C. Sproul answers the skeptical philosopher Anthony Flew, who speaks for Western intellectualism. Flew wrote a parable of two explorers who come upon a perfectly cultivated garden in the midst of an impenetrable rain forest. They wait to meet the gardener, but none comes. They string bells around the garden so they can hear if the gardener visits in the darkness, but the bells never sound. One of the explorers concludes that there is no gardener, the other that the gardener is invisible and immaterial.

What practical difference, argues Flew, is there between a God who is infinite, eternal, and invisible and no God at all? The difference, observes Sproul, is the *garden*. As we look down upon creation we see triune fingerprints everywhere. The creative work of the Father, Son, and Holy Spirit interweaves the threads of life as a master composer blends counterpoint harmony, so that the whole is far greater than the sum of its parts. Or, remember that chapter 4 of the *Westminster Confession of Faith* addressed the wonder: "It pleased God the Father, Son, and Holy Ghost, for the manifestation of the glory of his eternal power, wisdom, and goodness, in the beginning to create or make of nothing the world, and all things therein, whether visible or invisible, in the space of six days, and all very good." What is the proof of the Gardener? The bottom line is that there exists a garden. It is there. And it is very good.

Or it *was* very good, Mrs. Eddy notwithstanding.

Covenant of life and death

We Christians become overly sensitive in reacting to the argument that a good God would not allow evil to infect creation. I've heard it called the "fatal flaw" in our faith, and sometimes we sound as if we agree with that assessment and are intent on apologizing for God. Three notions have infected Christians' thinking:

1. Since sin entered the picture, there must have been an inherent weakness in God's plan.
2. The presence of evil obliges God to immediately take away all of its effects if he is all-powerful and all-loving.
3. Ultimate good must aim at the greatest happiness for the greatest number of people.

A flawed design?

Was there a flaw in the design? Consider the lives of the first humans. The *Larger Catechism*'s description with which we opened this chapter states that they had:

Nurturing environment

Our first parents were perfectly placed in a garden ideally suited to their needs and purpose (Genesis 1:26–31); theirs was a "paradise."

Significant work

They enjoyed employment for which they were perfectly equipped. They were given what has been called the *cultural mandate*—a mandate that all human culture still shares—to be fruitful through the bearing of and nurturing of children, and to care for the land. Work was no afterthought or punishment. Work fulfilled the joy of accomplishing praise to the Creator. Genesis 1:28 exults in the high calling of humanity.

Sufficient authority

That calling to "dress" the garden includes perfect authority over it (Genesis 1:29–30; 2:19–20). Every seed-bearing plant, every animal, every bird were Adam's for food and enjoyment. When the ancient Jews read that Adam gave names to the animals, they understood something we may not. In ancient culture authority and power in a person were symbolically expressed by the giving of a name. To name something denoted a right of authority over what was named. When God gave new names to certain biblical people he was indicating a new dimension of his involvement in their lives.

Satisfying relationships

Our parents enjoyed perfect fellowship (Genesis 2:18–25). As Adam named the creatures, God showed him that these beings would not fulfil his emotional needs. He required continual fellowship with God and with others of his own kind. The fullest expression of interpersonal fellowship was in the mutually completing companionship of man and wife as one flesh.

Refreshing relaxation and praise

Our parents knew seasons of energizing rest and worship (Genesis 2:2–3). Were Adam and Eve ever tired from their labors at the end of the week? Did they need a rhythm of work, rest, and centering on God? The language of Genesis strongly suggests an affirmative answer to both questions.

This is the plan—a life-giving agreement between God and his subjects. What was the weakness of such a *covenant of life*? Its only "weakness" was that God gave to his subjects the choice to love him or to reject him. Adam and Eve were free to trust and love God for who he was, or to selfishly reject him. Those who charge God with allowing evil and suffering to slip from Pandora's box are usually those who demand freedom to live as they please. The Bible identifies that freedom as the key that unlocked and threw open that evil.

Why didn't God intervene?

One of Walt Disney's most noteworthy cartoons is a short segment in his film *Fantasia*. Mickey Mouse is a young, impetuous apprentice to a powerful and wise sorcerer. As the strains of Paul Dukas's delightfully haunting music carry along the story, the sorcerer leaves his young apprentice in charge of caring for his workshop full of strange potions. He also leaves his book of magic spells within reach. Curious, anxious for a short-cut with his chores, and desiring quick knowledge without waiting for wisdom, Mickey tries out the spells. At first all goes splendidly. The broom comes to life and takes over on its own. The water buckets carry water without the apprentice's muscle-power. Unfortunately the apprentice's commands for stopping do not work nearly as well as those for starting. The animated helpers turn malevolent as action and music whirl out of control.

Just in time the sorcerer walks in, discovers what is going on, and uses his magic to set things to rights. The badly chastened apprentice has learned his lesson, and all live happily ever after.

That is not how it happened in Eden; God does not play the role of rescuing cavalry. Instead, he confronts his miserable little apprentices as they try to squirm out of their mess by casting blame on each other and their serpent co-conspirator (Genesis 3:7–13). Adam finds part of the fault in God for making him a very troublesome wife. All the while the pair is cowering behind leaves to cover their nakedness. The blessings of their covenant of life lie broken at their feet. Instead of sympathy, a stiff lecture, and a pat on the head, God pronounces doom, as he had promised he would if they disobeyed (Genesis 3:14–24). God's judgment included:

Cursed environment

They must leave paradise and face life and death on an unfriendly planet.

Cursed work

Work would be hard and unfulfilling, childbirth's joy mixed with agony. The task of the cultural mandate was not removed, but it would now be won only by sweat and pain.

Cursed authority

Humankind would retain authority, but no longer in smooth partnership. Walls rose to separate people, animals, and plants. The mutually accepted role of headship had been spurned by Adam. The role of mutually blessing partnership, with the husband leading the wife and following God, would now be replaced by a pattern of dissatisfaction with the roles God had given the sexes.

Cursed relationships

This strife between men and women, of course, has an impact on marriage and other interpersonal relationships from Cain and Abel through Democrats and Republicans (though thankfully without too much bloodshed in the latter case). Perhaps most painful is the immense wall between people and their God. From then on, a Mediator and the shedding of blood must stand between human sin and God's holiness. First would come sacrifices of animals, then the system of priests to intercede for the people, then a temple to symbolize both the connection and the great distance between God and humans.

Promised relaxation and praise

Notice that God did not take away the Sabbath blessing. As life becomes harder and God more distant, the Sabbath takes on new meaning in resting from labor and praising God and hoping for the full renewal under God's promise. That renewal comes in a new covenant to replace the broken covenant of life.

Look what had happened to the holiness of God's fallen image bearer, to the natural righteousness and knowledge of God of unfallen humanity. Remember that God will not—cannot—do what will make him less than infinite, eternal, and unchangeable in wisdom, power, holiness, justice, goodness, and truth. Suddenly the awful situation becomes clear. God would have ceased to be God had he simply waved his sorcerer's wand and cleaned up after his willful creatures. For, in fact, it was the sin of Adam and Eve that they wanted to be apprentices to Godhood. That option was not open to them. And God is no magician. He is God.

But could he not have foreseen what would happen and stopped Eve's grasping hand? God desired something more than coerced, resentful obedience. The prophet Micah expressed what God desired in this way (6:8): "He hath shewed thee, O man, what is good; and what doth the LORD require of thee, but to do justly, and to love mercy, and to walk humbly with thy God?"

As for his foresight, we know from our understanding of his omniscience that he certainly knew and took into account what would happen from the start of creation.

The ultimate good

But were his actions good or right? The question of ultimate good has bothered philosophers for millennia. Our egalitarian culture has made it almost an undeniable axiom of ethics that good is what brings the greatest happiness to the greatest number of people. This is a form of situation ethics, the view that the right response in any situation is the one that shows the most compassion for others. We will look more closely at the fallacy of this ethical standard in book 3.

God's ethical correctness was on trial that day in the garden. Had he acted as the good sorcerer instead of the holy God, humanity would not be better off today. They would have suffered the loss of God's essential being as holy and righteous and just. The garden might have remained theirs, but they would have shared it with the small god of the humanist. That loss of God's godness would have made Satan the victor and Eden a creation without a worthy Creator. It would essentially have differed little from hell. There was another road, full of pain and suffering, but vindicating God's integrity. That was to replace the covenant of life with a *covenant of grace*, when the serpent would strike at the heel of a second Adam, and he would crush the serpent's head (Genesis 3:14–15). Paul explains in Romans 5:12–19:

> Wherefore, as by one man sin entered into the world, and death by sin; and so death passed upon all men, for that all have sinned. . . . Therefore as by the offence of one judgment came upon all men to condemnation; even so by the righteousness of one the free gift came upon all men unto justification of life. For as by one man's disobedience many were made [appointed or declared] sinners, so by the obedience of one shall many be made [appointed or declared] righteous.

The great covenant of grace, and its promise of salvation in Jesus Christ alone, is the highest peak we can reach in our understanding of God, and the subject of book 2. We will not explore that peak just now, but we can stand on its majesty and look down on the world from its point of grandeur.

As we look down at the world we are not so far off as to miss the sight of bloody struggle that is still underway because of sin. We hear the sounds of spiritual warfare. God maintains control of this battle, and the final outcome in Christ no longer remains in doubt. But the battle continues to devastate human society and the natural world. The natural state of humanity was once "to do justly, and to love mercy, and to walk humbly with thy God." With sin in the picture:

There is none righteous, no, not one: There is none that understandeth, there is none that seeketh after God. They are all gone out of the way, they are together become unprofitable; there is none that doeth good, no, not one. [Romans 3:10–12]

That is a picture of what theologians call *radical depravity*. Unfortunately it is the real state of each unsaved person—what the *Westminster Shorter Catechism* calls a "state of sin and misery." Chapter 6 of the *Westminster Confession* spells it out:

By this sin they [our first parents] fell from their original righteousness and communion with God, and so became dead in sin, and wholly defiled in all the faculties and parts of soul and body.

They being the root of all mankind, the guilt of this sin was imputed, and the same death in sin and corrupted nature conveyed to all their prosperity descending from them by ordinary generation.

From this original corruption, whereby we are utterly indisposed, disabled and made opposite to all good, and wholly inclined to all evil, do proceed all actual transgressions.

At the naked feet of Adam, the covenant breaker, can be laid every act of oppression and suffering yet visited or ready to be visited upon this planet. It was an infinitely vile offense because it impugned the integrity and affronted the majestic prerogatives of an infinitely holy Being. And when we break any command of God are we doing less? As shameful as it makes me feel, I only see two differences between my acts of rebellion and Adam's. First, like Eve, I am not the direct head or administrator of the covenant between God and humanity. Adam was. Second, I know something about evil and its costs. I approach sin with eyes wide open.

In Psalm 51:4 King David asks God for forgiveness after he had committed adultery with another man's wife and then murdered the husband, one of his own trusted lieutenants, in a cover-up. Further, he had betrayed the trust of the nation, yet he says: "Against thee, *thee only*, have I sinned, and done this evil in thy sight." David could not have denied that his evil cost Bathsheba, Uriah, and Israel, but he understood that every crime—regardless of the human cost—ultimately stands committed against God's holiness. God is the ultimate victim, and the penalty for victimizing God is death. Who dares accuse God of being uncaring and unfair when we have seen what sin means in eternal perspective?

The way of the transgressor

Is depravity a reality? In 1648, ironically the year following the completion of the Westminster standards, the world turned a corner in its thinking about good and evil. That year the Treaty of Westphalia ended the Thirty Years War, an unspeakably cruel series of conflicts that devastated Europe as petty regional rulers fought for power and land. These rulers tried to legitimize their greed, however, by trumpeting that they were defending true Christianity against their heretical enemies. In the end there were no real winners, only war weary people who decided to enact a tolerance based upon apathy. They no longer cared who was right and wrong. Surely no faith was worth the price. Religion was to blame. If people minded their own business and quit worrying about right and wrong, everyone would be much happier and peaceful.

This was the hour of decision for the West. The men of faith who wrote the Westminster documents tried to turn their country toward the Bible's view of a desperately bent humanity and an utterly holy and merciful God. Most of the rest of the world turned toward the Enlightenment view that the human mind could reason itself out of depravity.

The Treaty of Westphalia sought to end the slaughter over absolutist beliefs. Our age seeks a new war on the absolutes themselves and those who say that absolutes do exist. Lately the catch-phrase has been "political correctness." As I understand what political correctness means, there is now an intolerance toward those who say that what I want to do might possibly be sinful. There is no truth versus error, no right and wrong, no evil versus good. Actually, the politically correct mentality declares that there is one evil—any narrow prudery that shakes its bony finger in my face and says, "I know you are having fun, so stop it right now!"

Against that attitude a wise man once looked at the facts: Some acts and thoughts are beneficial and helpful; other acts and thoughts are harmful to self and others. Further, some acts and thoughts have been condemned by the Creator of heaven and earth, and anyone who does or thinks them offends God and stands condemned. That wise man wrote: "Good understanding giveth favour: but the way of the transgressors is hard" (Proverbs 13:15). If there is no evil, or if absolutes are identified as the only evil, then there is no transgressor. There is nothing to transgress. Hence, there are no transgressors to have a hard life.

Case in point: The television program *Good Morning America* was filming in Sweden. One particular episode discussed the sexual freedom that exists in

Sweden. The film crew interviewed several people who agreed that young people "are going to do it anyway," so rather than force them to have sex in a car parked on lover's lane somewhere, they tell them to "bring the girl home where it's nice and safe; where you can take the proper precautions." Throughout the television program there was never the slightest hint that sexual relations outside marriage are immoral. They lamented the fact that it probably would be years before such "freedom" existed in America, because of the church.

A vice-president of one television network said that what disturbs him is not the immorality that exists in the entertainment media, but the amorality—the total ignoring of any moral standards whatsoever. We have come to joke about the people who appear on talk shows to talk about their involvement in every conceivable sort of immoral activity, without the slightest hint that they are doing anything wrong.

But the evidence suggests that there is a price to pay for amoral attitudes and immoral actions. In South Florida there are now at least twenty-six flagrant sexually-transmittable diseases, not including HIV. In a sermon at Coral Ridge Presbyterian Church I once mentioned that I had observed a young man in the congregation the week before who showed every sign of being in the final stages of the AIDS infection. At that time, just a few years ago, the tragic sight of these men and women who resemble a walking corpse was less common than it has become today. After the service the young man came up to me. He said, "You referred to me in your sermon this morning. I want you to know that last Sunday in the service I found salvation." Praise God. That man today is with his Lord. But salvation and redemption in the blood of Jesus Christ did not take away the consequences of his transgression in the flesh. His way was hard. Murderer Ted Bundy confessed Christ in a moving video with James Dobson just hours before he was strapped into the electric chair. If that confession was genuine, Ted Bundy stands equally forgiven with other redeemed sinners in heaven. But his addiction to pornography led him down a hard road to a hard end. Forgiven by God, he still had to pay the price in his body.

In his mercy God does withhold the physical judgment our sins deserve for a time. I am an example of his forbearance. I was converted when I was almost twenty-four years old. Before that time I lived the life of a promiscuous, unregenerate American heathen. Why did not I become infected with some disease or sink further and further into alcohol abuse or commit a crime deserving a lengthy imprisonment? I would *like* to tell you that there was something in me that made God withhold such judgments. In fact, it had nothing to do with my worthiness and everything to do with grace—God's sheer unmerited forbearance and love. When two people equally abuse themselves or others or God it seems unfair that one dies from his folly at age twenty and the other survives to become an octogenarian. But if God gave us what we deserve he would strike us all down immediately. He is merciful. But don't think you can toy with that mercy. The hard way of the eighty-year-old may be just as arduous a penalty for transgression as that of the man who died in his youth. And both will stand before God condemned for all eternity if they do not have a Savior. That is the way of all transgressors—a hard way indeed.

Groaning, joy, and a Redeemer

Scripture informs us of the consequences of sin and describes its victims. First, creation as a whole was victimized. Second, the breaking of the covenantal relationship so skewed human nature that unsaved people are unable to do anything *except* rebel against God. Third, while not totally gone, the mirror image of God we carry was beaten almost beyond recognition. Fourth, God not only is victimized by every sin; in his love he gave himself to *be* sin, taking on himself the infinite punishment for the infinite crime. God became a victim twice—in the garden and on the cross. That second time was when the mess left by the apprentice sorcerers was set aright and the covenant of grace fulfilled.

The groaning and joy of creation

Proverbs 13:15 not only tells the story of the results of sin today but the result of sin from the beginning. In fact, according to Romans 8:19–23 the way is hard for all creation because of sin. The effects of sin infected the good in which all things originally were created; all things experienced frustration:

> For the earnest expectation of the creature waiteth for the manifestation of the sons of God. For the creature was made subject to vanity, not willingly, but by reason of him who hath subjected the same in hope, Because the creature itself also shall be delivered from the bondage of corruption into the glorious liberty of the children of God. For we know that the whole creation groaneth and travaileth in pain together until now, and not only they, but ourselves also, which have the firstfruits of the Spirit, even we ourselves groan within ourselves, waiting for the adoption, to wit, the redemption of our body.

We did not fall alone. From the beginning the fate of inanimate creation was inextricably bound up with that of its caretakers. And creation's hope is through the redemption that happened on the cross. Someday it will be totally fulfilled when the angel will stand down from his guardhouse at the gate to Eden, and all will be renewed. As John mystically described that moment: "I saw a new heaven and a new earth: for the first heaven and the first earth were passed away" (Revelation 21:1a).

The groaning and joy of the redeemed

John goes on to say that renewed creation will have no "sea" (Revelation 21:1b). In Scripture the sea tends to symbolize that which separates people from people and people from God. Today, like creation, we groan. Some room for argument exists as to whether Paul in Romans 7 is talking about the plight of the unsaved or his continuing frustrations with sin. Whomever he addresses, I also feel frustrated that:

> For that which I do I allow not: for what I would, that do I not; but what I hate, that do I. . . . For I know that in me (that is, in my flesh,) dwelleth no good thing: for to will is present with me; but how to perform that which is good I find not. For the good that I would I do not: but the evil which I would not, that I do. [Romans 7:15–19]

Yet the person in Christ has an answer to this frustration. The depraved Paul shouts: "O wretched man that I am! who shall deliver me from the body of this death?" (Romans 7:24). The redeemed Paul already knows the only answer: "I thank God through Jesus Christ our Lord" (7:25).

The whole message of the Bible is one of *generation*, *degeneration*, and *regeneration*. The human race still bears the image of God, but twisted and perverted. It is like a Cadillac that has rolled off the production line at General Motors, been driven a few miles, and then rolled over a 500-foot cliff. There is a Cadillac at the bottom, but who will argue that it is the same as it was? The wrecked Cadillac needs to be towed into the garage, have its fenders and doors pounded out, the frame straightened, and the motor repaired. Humanity is a noble wreck, and that alone is the reason for its sin and despair.

The three transforming tasks

For the one who has gone from degeneration to regeneration, however, God's glorious, ever-renewing purpose awaits. Remember what we know of that purpose:

1. Our chief end is to glorify and enjoy God—both now and forever.
2. Our initial instructions, given at the dawn of creation, were to be fruitful, to multiply, to replenish and subdue the earth, and to rule its creatures. All humanity, all cultures, both Christian and non-Christian, own this cultural mandate. Only the Christian, however, can appreciate why we own it.
3. Jesus gave us new marching orders, a Great Commission, at the dawn of new creation. Jesus said:

All power is given unto me in heaven and in earth. Go ye therefore, and teach all nations, baptizing them in the name of the Father, and of the Son, and of the Holy Ghost: Teaching them to observe all things whatsoever I have commanded you: and, lo, I am with you alway, even unto the end of the world. [Matthew 28:18b–20]

How do we participate in those three life-transforming tasks? We must get to know the Father, Son, and Holy Spirit as revealed in Scripture. That can only truly happen as we realize that God's plan for history did include the fall into sin. A kingdom of the redeemed was established from the dawn of time (Matthew 25:34). That kingdom was established in Jesus Christ from the beginning (Ephesians 1:4). Entrance to that kingdom was always, is now, and ever will be based on the sacrifice of Jesus Christ for our sins. That sacrifice was promised at the fall but it had already been planned as the way to God:

> Forasmuch as ye know that ye were not redeemed with corruptible things, as silver and gold, from your vain conversation received by tradition from your fathers; But with the precious blood of Christ, as of a lamb without blemish and without spot: Who verily was foreordained before the foundation of the world, but was manifest in these last times for you, Who by him do believe in God, that raised him up from the dead, and gave him glory; that your faith and hope might be in God. [1 Peter 1:18–21]

It is those who believe Jesus is God, who died and arose in victory from the grave, and who accept his authority as Lord who have escaped the curse of our first parents. It is those depraved but delivered people whose names are "written in the book of life of the Lamb slain from the foundation of the world" (Revelation 13:8).

Redeemed, we still are like that sadly mangled Cadillac that has gone over the cliff. We must be towed to the garage, and the effects of sin must be hammered out and our frame straightened before we can commune with God and glorify and enjoy him. Within the divine body shop we study God's revelation, pray to him, worship him, and follow his commandments, giving thanks for his great glory. And we begin the joy of obeying his Great Commission—making disciples like ourselves, and representing Christ in all the spheres of life, from marriage and parenting to schools and government, music, literature, art, and business.

When our greatest purpose is to offer our minds to knowing God more fully and our lives in testimony to God's lordship over all, then we have truly begun to glorify God and enjoy him forever.

Come with me. Let us walk on together, pilgrims on the adventure of an eternity—transformed and transforming people who know their God.

Study Guide

Introduction

Words to define

belief   religion   soteriology
truth   theology   ethics
creed   orthodoxy

Points to ponder

1. Transforming belief is based on scriptural facts but also involves an emotional commitment that is focused in someone or something.

2. Transforming faith in Jesus Christ is both a religion and a relationship.

3. Each person has a creed, although many have not consciously thought it through.

Questions to answer

1. What did the man who brought his child to Jesus mean when he said, "I believe. Help thou my unbelief"?

2. Is anything wrong with making reason the yardstick for determining truth? With making emotions or feelings the yardstick?

3. What transformed Jesus' disciples into the men they became in the early church?

4. Is there a difference between the belief that the Bible becomes truth and the belief that it is truth?

5. Can something be inspiring and sound like truth, yet be wrong and evil?

6. What is the purpose of a confession of faith?

7. Describe the relationship between human beings and God:

    a. as he created us to be

    b. as we became

    c. as we can be in Jesus Christ

Notebook

Begin a notebook for recording answers to questions and your responses to the ideas addressed in the coming chapters. Write a paragraph summing up your conception of God. Leave space for adding thoughts from other chapters. Does your idea of God seem adequate?

Chapter 1: Quest for Life

Words to define

epistemology   primacy

truth assumptions   glorify

ultimate truth   confession

worldview   catechism

dogmatism

Points to ponder

1. The *Westminster Confession of Faith* was originally followed by most Protestants, especially Presbyterians, Congregationalists, and Baptists (the latter two with some reservations about the nature of the church). Since the early 1800s the tendency in the church has been to downplay the importance of confessional statements of belief.

2. Ultimate truths make our own ideas of truth irrelevant. They are true whether we like it or not.

3. God has revealed to us in Scripture the ultimate truths about himself—truths worth living and dying for. The *Westminster Confession* summarizes these truths.

Questions to answer

1. Evaluate the bishop's three guides for deciding whether active homosexuality should be accepted as a Christian lifestyle. Why should Scripture carry any more weight than tradition or decisions by leaders?

2. What are some other guides people follow? Why should Christians have a different set of guides than does anyone else?

3. Why is the search for significance so important to each man or woman?

4. Is anything really wrong with a self-glorifying philosophy? What does such a philosophy give? What does it lack?

5. Why haven't the ultimate truths of Scripture transformed the pagan culture of the West? What is the place of Christians in government and society? The place of the church? The place of you as a citizen?

6. What does it mean to glorify and enjoy God?

7. Can anyone avoid walking by faith of some sort? Why or why not?

8. In what ways does the story of the blind man on the precipice illustrate the lifestyle of the world?

Notebook

If you have not completed the list of blessings that belong to the Christian found in Ephesians 1:3–14 do so now. By each gift, note a way that life is transformed in those to whom God has given such a blessing. If you have come to Christ with hands open and outstretched, what can those blessings mean to you this week? By what faith are you now setting the course of your life?

Chapter 2: The Only Rule

Words to define

general revelation   sanctify
special revelation   inspiration
authority   prophecy
Scripture

Points to ponder

1. Creation reveals God, but Scripture alone reveals the character and will of God.

2. While the Bible sometimes speaks in fictional parables or metaphors, it must be true in all of its factual statements or it is fraudulent and worthless.

3. The Holy Spirit bears witness to the divine authority of Scripture and makes that truth live in the hearts of God's people.

Questions to answer

1. Why is it so important that we be established in the truth of God?

2. How do the Bible's claims about itself differ from those of other religions' sacred writings?

3. In what ways does human sinfulness make it more difficult to know God and his will through Scripture and creation?

4. Is it really so important that the Bible contains no factual errors or contradictions?

5. Can the books of the Scripture really be "God-breathed," or inspired? Weren't they written by people?

6. If God is a King who speaks to his subjects, as J. I. Packer wrote, what does that mean in our lives?

7. How do the prophecies in the Bible compare and contrast with the predictions of today's "prophets"?

8. What is the work of the Holy Spirit in relation to Scripture?

Notebook

In your own words, write down what you believe about the Bible. What arguments would you use to defend your beliefs? Does your understanding of Scripture give a basis for knowing how to glorify God and enjoy him?

Chapter 3: A God Suppressed

Words to define

infinite
suppression
evidence
materialism
cosmology

teleology
causation
creation
evolution

Points to ponder

1. Transforming faith rests on two pillars: (1) confidence in Scripture as God's trustworthy, authoritative, and complete revelation; (2) confidence in an infinite, eternal, and unchangeable God who reveals himself in creation and providence.

2. Men and women suppress knowledge of a transforming God because they want no absolute truth to demand their obedience.

3. As science reveals more of the intricacies of creation, its complexity and obvious design make the faith of unbelief difficult. Yet the unbelieving heart filters out the truth and holds fast to the unbelievable lie.

Questions to answer

1. Why is an accurate understanding about Scripture so vital to true faith? What information must Scripture give us about God in order for us to build a life-transforming faith?

2. Does the tendency to suppress truth extend to Christians? What are some reasons churches face such rancor and division over the doctrines of Scripture and of God?

3. What must the person who denies God believe about life and his or her place in it? What other doctrines are part of the unbeliever's statement of faith?

4. Does the description of fallen humanity in Romans 1 justify the *Westminster Confession*'s statement: "We are utterly indisposed, disabled, and made opposite to all good, and wholly inclined to all evil"?

5. If the Bible is not a book of science and the people of Bible times are looked down on as "prescientific," why should we care whether science agrees with what the Bible says about creation?

6. Looking at the balance and symmetry that extends from the subatomic level to the galaxies, describe God revealed in nature.

7. What is wrong with the argument that the God who created the universe could not be concerned about how I live?

Notebook

Imagine that you are seeing a baby for the first time. Step into Whitaker Chambers's shoes as a new father and notice the delicate beauty and design of this infant body. Can God be mirrored in the human form? List some ways your own life needs to mirror God's providence to complement what he already displays in your body.

Chapter 4: God Who Grows

Words to define

infinite	omniscient	immanence
eternal	omnipotent	transcendent
immutable		

Points to ponder

1. We grow in transforming faith to the extent that we allow God's Word to transform our conception of who he is as our God.

2. God is only limited in that he cannot do anything that would make him less than God.

3. God is infinite, eternal, and unchangeable in wisdom, power, holiness, justice, goodness, and truth.

Questions to answer

1. What do the names by which God is called in Scripture reveal to us about his character?

2. What did John Calvin mean when he said that we cannot know ourselves without a knowledge of God?

3. Does the fact that God is a Spirit, without body parts or passions, lend credibility to the atheist who says that he does not exist? What is the difference between God as a Spirit, and angels and human beings as spiritual beings?

4. Can God create a stone so large he cannot lift it?

5. What divine attributes did Jesus leave when he became a human being? What divine attributes remained his, even as he lay in the manger of Bethlehem? Was the risen and ascended Jesus more than he had been before he became a human?

6. In what ways is God unchanging? Then how can Scripture speak of God changing his mind?

7. How should our understanding of God's omnipotence and omniscience transform our thoughts as we communicate with him in prayer?

Notebook

Job 42:5–6 makes the point that it is one thing to hear about God, but quite another to encounter him in the furnace of affliction or in the realization that no one can come before his infinite holiness without the infinite sacrifice of Jesus Christ. Write about the moment that you first remember being aware of God in a personal way. Can your encounters with the infinite, eternal, and unchangeable God be shared with a friend or relative who does not know him?

Chapter 5: The Absurd Trinity

Words to define

theism
monotheism
polytheism
deism

pantheism
atheism
rationalism
idealism

theological
   liberalism
arianism
neo-orthodoxy

Points to ponder

1. God is not like anything else in our experience.

2. The history of modern philosophy is the story of human rebellion against the idea of a triune God who is both immanent and transcendent.

3. The great struggle of our day is to return our churches to the doctrine of God revealed in Scripture.

Questions to answer

1. Why is the doctrine of the Trinity so important to Christian faith? What can God do as Son and as Holy Spirit that are distinct from his being as Creator and Lord of the universe?

2. What does the father-son metaphor tell us about the relationship between God the Creator and God the Redeemer?

3. Why is the god of deism safer than the triune God of Christianity?

4. Why did rationalist philosophy and Christianity battle so long and hard over whether God can be known and over whether he revealed himself in Scripture?

5. What changed in the outlook of science that it moved from being a tool of discovery of the work of God to being a pulpit for denying God's reality?

6. Why is New Age theology so fashionable and pervasive in today's society?

7. What is wrong with saying that we come to God by making a blind leap of faith?

8. How does the Trinity meet us in our everyday lives? If Jesus is in heaven, is it wrong to sing that Jesus, rather than the Holy Spirit, "came into my heart"?

Notebook

It is popular today to seek positions from which to dialog with people of other faiths. Think through what limits Christians should set on such dialog. Can we work together for mutual social and political reforms? Can we help one another combat injustice and prejudice? Should we worship together, pray together, or look for ways to make our religions compatible with one another?

Chapter 6: The God Revolution

Words to define

worldview	evolution	image of God
creation	materialism	cultural mandate

Points to ponder

1. Materialism and theism are the alternative world-views that vie for the allegiance of the world today. The materialist's view of humanity, if consistent, can ultimately see no intrinsic value in human life.

2. None of today's moral issues are new or unique. What is unusual, and perhaps unique, is the acceptance

and even the valuing of the very behaviors that have caused other societies to disintegrate.

3. The God who created from nothing also re-creates sinners into renewed children who are able to be fruitful.

Questions to answer

1. Why cannot a pro-abortion activist and an anti-abortion Christian activist talk to one another with any significant mutual understanding?

2. Why does accepting the theory of materialistic evolution as fact guarantee the devaluing of humanity? What are some of the ways people are degraded in this theory?

3. How can the theory of evolution be called a hoax when its truth is assumed by many of the most brilliant scientists and philosophers?

4. What lessons might we draw from the manifestation of vital Christianity in the former Soviet republics? Is the Romanians' passion for Christ related to the years they spent under an atheistic system?

5. If Ernest Gordon is correct that education is "an expression of the prevailing culture," what must occur before Western education can again become functional? What can the Christian church contribute to society and culture because we know the truth of creation and follow the Creator?

6. In the midst of cultural crisis, what hope and cultural mandate can we draw from such passages as 1 Chronicles 16:25, Romans 8, Revelation 21:5, and other passages that speak of God's re-creating power?

7. Given the state of society and culture, is this the time to withdraw and wait for God's intervention, or does the cultural mandate call Christians to sat-

urate the arts, education, business, and other spheres of life with an alternative to materialism? If the latter, how does one go about subduing and ruling now?

Notebook

The world of the twentieth century is usually thought of as the grand victory of the Enlightenment and the Industrial Revolution. Yet Charles Colson in his book *Against the Night* warns that we have entered a new Dark Ages. Is such pessimism justified? Is there corresponding reason for optimism and even excitement?

Chapter 7: Plan, Power, and Providence

Words to define

sovereignty	futility	miracles
providence	fatalism	lordship

Points to ponder

1. The sovereignty of God extends to every facet of life, yet each human being does exactly what he or she wants in any given situation.

2. God rules through his acts of creation and providence. "He orders and executes His work in the most excellent and just manner, even when devils and wicked men act unjustly."

3. As ruler, God demands the right of lordship over each human being; no man or woman is truly free from the lordship of God.

Questions to answer

1. Why is the doctrine of God's sovereign direction so widely disputed, even among Christians?

2. What keeps me from being the "master of my fate and the captain of my soul"? Is it God who limits human freedom, or is it something else?

3. Can God preserve creation, govern creation, and govern human thoughts and actions without being blamable for the evil in the world?

4. How can we explain as Christians the extraordinary events we call "miracles" that are recorded in Scripture?

5. Is it possible to accept Jesus as Savior but not accept him as personal Lord and Master? How can subjection to God be a blessing?

6. What do we gain in exchange for turning over to God the prerogatives of lordship? What do we lose?

7. When will Christ's rule over the earth begin? When will it be complete?

Notebook

Think back to a time when life seemed out of control. Can you see now the hand of God preserving and directing in what happened? What came out of that time: emotional or spiritual maturity, perhaps, or the ability to minister to others in a similar situation? Was the outcome what you would have asked for, or did God answer in a way far beyond what you would have imagined? Do some questions about what happened remain unanswered? If so, have you come to the point at which you can trust without total understanding?

Chapter 8: The Sorcerer's Apprentice

Words to define

covenant of life   degeneration
radical depravity   regeneration
covenant of grace   fall
transgression

Points to ponder

1. Adam was created for fellowship with God and placed in a world that was "very good." His environment, work, authority, relationships, and refreshment were perfectly designed to fulfil his needs.

2. The fall into sin erected barriers of alienation separating Adam from God, from other people, from himself, and from his purpose for existing.

3. In Christ we can move from degeneration to regeneration and participate in three transforming tasks of the kingdom of God.

Questions to answer

1. What did God give to humanity in the first covenantal relationship of the garden?

2. Why did not God intervene to keep Adam and Eve from rebelling against him?

3. Was death the only penalty that could be levied against humankind? Why couldn't God simply undo the damage that had been done and immediately restore Adam to fellowship with him?

4. What happened to humanity as a race in the "state of sin and misery"?

5. If King David seduced Bathsheba and killed her husband, why does he say in Psalm 51 that his crime was a sin against God alone? What is meant by the statement that God was a victim of sin twice?

6. What are some ways that creation groans because of the fall into sin? Is there hope for a renewed creation?

7. Why did Christ, the second person of the Trinity, have to come to earth as a human, suffer, and die to redeem those in a state of sin and misery?

Notebook

Review what you have read and written about God through this series of lessons. Have you come to a point in your life where you are able to stand before him forgiven in Jesus Christ? If not, today is the day you can begin the three transforming tasks described in this chapter. Christ has paid the infinite price so that you can repent and turn from sin to transforming faith in Jesus as your Savior and Lord. Book 2 will tell you more about what this means. If you have begun those tasks in your life already, write a prayer of praise, asking God to lead you on to glorify and enjoy him ever more fully.